C000156990

DECADENCE

DESSERTS BY PHILIP JOHNSON

DECADENCE

DESSERTS BY PHILIP JOHNSON

MURDOCH BOOKS

CONTENTS

Special thanks to my wife Shirley and son Oliver, who understand that when I say I'm going to be home I'm just joking.

To Tracey Rayner, my manager, friend, conscience and disobedient daughter, all rolled into one — I couldn't do it without you!

To Kristie Rickman, who worked with me as an enthusiastic apprentice when we first opened e'cco and has returned as a gifted pastry chef. The guys in the kitchen joke that this has been the easiest book I've done yet.

To Mathias Andersson, my head chef, who along with Nik, Sam and their team keep things running while I'm often away.

To Tanya, Mel, Alan and the floor team — good food is only half the equation.

To photographer Jared Fowler, for the amazing images, and stylist Cherise Koch, for her understanding every time I changed my mind.

And thanks especially to Kay Scarlett and Juliet Rogers of Murdoch Books, and my editor Katri Hilden and her team for their unwavering support.

I've often read about the debate on cooking — is it science or is it art? I think the simplest way to think of it is that art begins where science ends.

Whether you believe their secret lies in art or alchemy, sweet things are certainly one of life's most dependable pleasures. I was reminded of this recently when I ate an eccles cake, a rich, fruity delicacy from northern England that I used to make with my grandmother as a young boy.

This time it was served in the traditional way, with a crumbly cheese, but it took me straight back to those childhood days where my passion for desserts first began, when I loved dabbling with other simple yet luscious desserts such as pavlova and self-saucing chocolate puddings.

Years later, I completed my apprenticeship and was living in London, where I spent many of my days off working in the pastry section of the fabled Ritz Hotel, purely to gain knowledge. The insights I received there have stayed with me throughout all my years of cooking.

Desserts have long been a passion of mine and had it been my choice, although I was never trained in pastry, my first book would have been about desserts. This book is number five so I've finally made it! As they say, you need to walk before you can run. Patience is a virtue, and as a chef, timing is everything.

Just like entrées and mains, desserts are a fine balance of textures, flavours and temperatures. They are also an occasion for a chef to show restraint. That may sound like a contradiction, but the final course shouldn't be the one that leaves you feeling like you'll never eat again. It should be the perfect end to the perfect meal, before the coffee arrives.

At e'cco, we obviously spend a lot of time and effort getting our desserts as perfect as we can. But then we like to get them on the plate and let them speak for themselves.

While our desserts often draw praise for their simplicity, our guests are also often surprised to find a combination of sweet, tart and exotic flavours.

As a chef, that's what excites me the most about creating desserts. Having the freedom to be a little more adventurous, yet finding that exquisite balance, inviting diners to surrender to feelings of pure indulgence and decadence. I hope this book helps you enjoy many such moments.

Philip Johnson
e'cco

CRAZY FOR CHOCOLATE

If you're a serious chocoholic and want to create a dessert
'to die for', make sure you use good-quality couverture chocolate
in the following recipes. For me, couverture is the king of chocolate.
Rich, glossy and beautifully textured, it simply has no peers, and
will make all the difference to these decadent desserts.

Flourless chocolate cake with fresh raspberries & cream

Serves 8

400 g (14 oz/2²/₃ cups) chopped
  good-quality dark (bittersweet)
  chocolate, such as couverture
6 eggs
95 g (3¹/₄ oz/¹/₂ cup) muscovado
  sugar (or dark brown sugar if
  unavailable)
2 tablespoons dark rum
250 ml (9 fl oz) thick (double/heavy)
  cream

250 ml (9 fl oz/1 cup) pouring
  (whipping) cream, whipped
fresh raspberries, to decorate
icing (confectioners') sugar, for
  dusting

Preheat the oven to 180°C (350°F/Gas 4). Grease and line the base and side of a 26 cm (10¹/2 inch) spring-form cake tin with baking paper.

Put the chocolate in a heatproof bowl over a saucepan of simmering water and allow to melt, stirring occasionally, until smooth. Remove from the heat and allow to cool slightly.

Put the eggs, sugar and rum in a separate heatproof bowl over a saucepan of simmering water, whisking constantly until the mixture doubles in volume. Remove from the heat. Fold in the cooled chocolate, then fold in the thick cream, mixing well to combine.

Pour the cake mixture into the prepared tin. Half-fill a large roasting tin with hot water and place on the bottom rack of the oven. (This will create a steam effect in the oven to help the cake cook evenly.) Transfer the cake to the oven and bake for 40 minutes, or until a skewer inserted into the centre of the cake comes out clean. Allow the cake to cool in the tin before turning out.

Top the cake with the whipped cream, decorate with raspberries and dust with icing sugar.

Chocolate marquise with crème anglaise, pistachios & almond tuiles

Serves 8

200 g (7 oz) unsalted butter, diced

300 g (10¹/₂ oz/2 cups) chopped good-quality dark (bittersweet) chocolate, such as couverture

500 ml (17 fl oz/2 cups) pouring (whipping) cream

220 g (7^3/$_4$ oz/2^3/$_4$ cups) icing (confectioners') sugar, plus extra, for dusting

6 egg yolks

85 g (3 oz/^{2}/$_3$ cup) unsweetened cocoa powder, sifted

2 tablespoons Cointreau

a half-quantity of tuile mixture (Basics, page 183)

55 g (2 oz/scant ^{2}/$_3$ cup) flaked almonds

1 quantity of crème anglaise (Basics, page 178)

100 g (3^1/$_2$ oz/^{3}/$_4$ cup) shelled unsalted pistachio nuts, blanched, skinned and roughly chopped

Put the butter and chocolate in a heatproof bowl over a saucepan of simmering water and allow to melt, stirring occasionally, until smooth. Remove from the heat and set aside to cool. Meanwhile, whisk the cream with 4 tablespoons of the icing sugar until soft peaks form. Set aside.

In the bowl of an electric mixer, whisk the egg yolks with the remaining icing sugar until thick and pale. Add the cocoa powder and Cointreau and mix well to combine. Fold in the cooled chocolate mixture, then the whipped cream.

Rinse a 25 x 12 cm (10 x 4^1/$_2$ inch) loaf (bar) tin with water and line with plastic wrap, allowing a 4 cm (1^1/$_2$ inch) overhang around the sides. Pour the chocolate marquise mixture into the tin, then tap the tin lightly on a work surface to settle the mixture. Gently cover the top with the overhanging plastic wrap and refrigerate overnight, or until set.

Preheat the oven to 160°C (315°F/Gas 2–3). Prepare the tuile mixture as directed on page 183.

Draw three 10 cm (4 inch) circles on a sheet of baking paper and invert the paper over a baking tray. Repeat with another sheet of baking paper and baking tray.

Using a spatula, smear a thin layer of batter onto each circle and sprinkle with the flaked almonds. Bake for 3–5 minutes, or until brown at the edges and golden in the centre. Remove from the oven and, working quickly using a clean palette knife or spatula, carefully remove one tuile and gently roll into a cigar shape. Repeat with the second and third tuile — if they become too hard to remove, return the tray briefly to the oven to soften. Repeat with the remaining batter. Allow to cool, then store in an airtight container until required.

Turn the cold chocolate marquise out of the loaf tin onto a cutting board. Using a hot knife, cut it into slices about 1.5 cm (^{5}/$_8$ inch) thick and arrange two slices in the centre of each serving plate. Spoon the crème anglaise around and scatter with the pistachios. Serve with the almond tuiles, dusted with extra icing sugar.

Chocolate & hazelnut ice cream sandwich

Serves 6

1 quantity of chocolate and hazelnut
  ice cream (page 164)

FRANGELICO SYRUP
250 g (9 oz/heaped 1 cup) caster
  (superfine) sugar
100 ml (3^1/$_2$ fl oz) freshly squeezed
  orange juice
100 ml (3^1/$_2$ fl oz) Frangelico (hazelnut
  liqueur)

CHOCOLATE WAFERS
50 g (1^3/$_4$ oz) unsalted butter,
  softened
50 g (1^3/$_4$ oz/^{1}/$_4$ cup) caster
  (superfine) sugar
2 tablespoons corn syrup
2 egg whites, lightly beaten
75 g (2^1/$_2$ oz) plain (all-purpose) flour
1 tablespoon unsweetened cocoa
  powder

icing (confectioners') sugar, for
  dusting
40 g (1^1/$_2$ oz/^{1}/$_3$ cup) hazelnuts,
  roasted, skinned and roughly
  chopped

Prepare the chocolate and hazelnut ice cream as directed. Once fully churned, spoon the ice cream into a shallow tray to a depth of 1 cm (^{1}/2 inch), then freeze.

To make the Frangelico syrup, combine the sugar and 125 ml (4 fl oz/^{1}/2 cup) water in a saucepan over medium heat and stir until the sugar has dissolved. Bring to the boil and boil, without stirring, until the syrup becomes a dark golden colour. Immediately remove from the heat and very carefully, as hot caramel spits, add the orange juice. Return the pan to low heat, add the Frangelico and stir until smooth. If the caramel is too thick, add a little more water. Allow to cool, then refrigerate until required.

Preheat the oven to 160°C (315°F/Gas 2–3). Grease and line several baking trays with baking paper.

To make the chocolate wafers, cream the butter and sugar together in the bowl of an electric mixer until light and pale. Whisk in the corn syrup, then the egg whites. Sift together the flour and cocoa powder, then fold into the creamed butter mixture.

Spread a thin, even layer of the wafer mixture over the prepared trays. Bake for 8–10 minutes, or until golden.

While still hot, cut the wafers into 10 cm (4 inch) squares (you will need 18 altogether) and allow to cool on the tray — the wafers will crack if you try to cut them once they are cold. Store in an airtight container until required.

Cut the ice cream into 8 cm (3^1/4 inch) squares. Place a wafer on each serving plate and top with a square of ice cream. Top with another wafer and another ice cream square, finishing with a wafer on top. Dust with icing sugar and scatter with the hazelnuts. Drizzle the Frangelico syrup around the plate.

Strawberry & chocolate 'lollipops'

Makes about 48

a half-quantity of strawberry sorbet (made using the fruit sorbet recipe on page 158 — or use a good-quality store-bought sorbet)
300 g (10$^1/_2$ oz/2 cups) chopped good-quality dark (bittersweet) chocolate, such as couverture

Line several baking trays with baking paper.

Use a melon baller to shape the sorbet into balls, then place on the baking trays. Insert a toothpick into each ball to make a 'lollipop'. Turn the freezer to the coldest setting, if possible, then freeze the lollipops overnight to set.

Put the chocolate in a heatproof bowl over a saucepan of simmering water and allow to melt, stirring occasionally, until smooth. Remove from the heat and allow to cool to room temperature.

One by one, dip the sorbet balls into the cooled chocolate so they are completely coated. Gently place the lollipops back on the lined trays and return to the freezer for the chocolate to set.

Remove the lollipops from the freezer 5–10 minutes before serving. The sorbet will soften slightly so the lollipops will 'explode' in your mouth!

Steamed chocolate & rum puddings

Serves 6

CHOCOLATE SAUCE
225 g (8 oz/1¾ cups) grated
   good-quality dark (bittersweet)
   chocolate, such as couverture
50 g (1¾ oz/¼ cup) caster
   (superfine) sugar
100 ml (3½ fl oz) pouring (whipping)
   cream

CHOCOLATE & RUM PUDDINGS
180 g (6 oz) store-bought chocolate
   sponge cake, crumbled to resemble
   breadcrumbs
90 g (3¼ oz/scant 1 cup) ground
   almonds
35 g (1¼ oz/heaped ¼ cup)
   unsweetened cocoa powder
2 tablespoons dark rum
150 g (5½ oz) unsalted butter,
   softened
70 g (2½ oz/scant ⅓ cup) caster
   (superfine) sugar
6 eggs, separated
100 g (3½ oz/⅔ cup) good-quality
   dark (bittersweet) chocolate melts
   (buttons), such as couverture
70 g (2½ oz/scant ⅓ cup) caster
   (superfine) sugar, extra

pouring (whipping) cream, to serve

To make the chocolate sauce, put the chocolate, sugar and 350 ml (12 fl oz) water in a heavy-based saucepan over medium heat, stirring constantly with a wooden spoon until the chocolate melts and the sugar dissolves. Bring to the boil, then reduce the heat and simmer for 10 minutes. Remove from the heat and skim the surface to remove any impurities. Stir in the cream, then strain through a fine sieve. Set aside to cool completely, then cover and refrigerate until required.

Preheat the oven to 200°C (400°F/Gas 6). Lightly grease six 125 ml (4 fl oz/½ cup) metal dariole moulds or ramekins.

To make the chocolate and rum puddings, combine the sponge crumbs, ground almonds and cocoa powder in a large bowl. Sprinkle with the rum.

In the bowl of an electric mixer, cream the butter and sugar together until light and pale. Add the egg yolks, one at a time, beating well after each addition. Stir in the sponge mixture, then fold in the chocolate melts (these will melt through the pudding during cooking).

In the bowl of an electric mixer, whisk the egg whites until soft peaks form, then gradually add the extra sugar and continue to whisk until all the sugar is used.

Carefully fold the beaten egg whites into the sponge mixture — the batter will be quite firm.

Spoon the pudding mixture into the prepared moulds. Sit the moulds in a large roasting tin and pour in enough boiling water to come halfway up the side of the moulds. Cover the moulds with a large sheet of baking paper, then cover the tray with foil. Bake for 25–30 minutes, or until the puddings spring back when touched.

Remove the puddings from the roasting tin. Run a paring knife around the edge of each dariole mould to loosen each pudding, then turn out onto a wire rack.

Gently reheat the chocolate sauce. Serve the warm puddings drizzled with the warm chocolate sauce and cream.

Chocolate, Kahlua & savoiardi torte

Serves 12

225 g (8 oz/1^1/$_2$ cups) chopped
  good-quality dark (bittersweet)
  chocolate, such as couverture
50 g (1^3/$_4$ oz) unsalted butter,
  chopped
2 tablespoons instant coffee powder
50 g (1^3/$_4$ oz/heaped ^{1}/$_3$ cup) raisins
50 g (1^3/$_4$ oz/^{1}/$_3$ cup) hazelnuts,
  roasted, skinned and roughly
  chopped
60 ml (2 fl oz/^{1}/$_4$ cup) Kahlua
150 ml (5 fl oz) pouring (whipping)
  cream, lightly whipped
250 g (9 oz) savoiardi (lady fingers/
  sponge finger biscuits), chopped
  (see Note)

unsweetened cocoa powder,
  for dusting

Line a 26 cm (10^1/2 inch) spring-form cake tin with plastic wrap, leaving a 4 cm (1^1/2 inch) overhang around the side.

Put the chocolate and butter in a heatproof bowl over a saucepan of simmering water and allow to melt, stirring occasionally, until smooth. Add the coffee powder, stirring well to dissolve. Remove from the heat.

Add the raisins, hazelnuts and Kahlua and mix well to combine. Allow to cool to room temperature.

Fold the whipped cream and savoiardi into the cooled chocolate mixture, then spoon the mixture into the prepared tin, pushing the top down gently using the back of a spoon. Gently cover the top with the overhanging plastic wrap and refrigerate for several hours, preferably overnight.

Dust the torte with cocoa powder, cut into thin wedges and serve.

NOTE: You can use ready-made savoiardi for this recipe, or see our recipe on page 144. This torte is very rich and is best served as a *petit four* with coffee.

Coffee, chocolate & almond meringue cake

Serves 8

ALMOND MERINGUE
9 egg whites
500 g (1 lb 2 oz/2 heaped cups) caster (superfine) sugar
175 g (6 oz/1 3/4 cups) ground almonds

COFFEE CHOCOLATE FILLING
250 ml (9 fl oz/1 cup) hot espresso or strong plunger coffee
400 g (14 oz/2 2/3 cups) chopped good-quality dark (bittersweet) chocolate, such as couverture
6 eggs, separated
80 g (2 3/4 oz/1/3 cup) caster (superfine) sugar

unsweetened cocoa powder, for dusting
lightly whipped cream, to serve

Preheat the oven to 120°C (235°F/Gas 1/2). Draw three 26 cm (10 1/2 inch) circles on a sheet of baking paper and invert the paper over three baking trays.

To make the almond meringue, whisk the egg whites in the bowl of an electric mixer until stiff peaks form. Gradually add the sugar and continue to whisk until all the sugar is used. Fold in the ground almonds, then spoon into a piping (icing) bag with a plain nozzle. Working from the centre of the circle on each baking paper sheet, pipe the meringue in an even circular motion until you reach the outer edge of the circle. Bake for 40 minutes, then turn the oven off and allow to dry in the oven for about 1 hour.

To make the coffee chocolate filling, put the coffee and chocolate in a small saucepan over medium heat and stir to dissolve the chocolate. Remove from the heat and transfer to a large bowl. Allow to cool slightly, then whisk in the egg yolks.

In the bowl of an electric mixer, whisk the egg whites until soft peaks form, then gradually add the sugar and continue to whisk until all the sugar is used.

Carefully fold half the beaten egg whites into the cooled chocolate mixture. Fold in the remaining beaten egg whites until well combined, then refrigerate in an airtight container until required.

To assemble the cake, spread half the coffee chocolate filling over one meringue disc. Place a second meringue disc on top. Spread with the remaining coffee chocolate filling and top with the third meringue disc. Dust with cocoa powder, cut into wedges and serve with a generous spoonful of whipped cream.

Bittersweet chocolate & Cointreau tart

Serves 8

450 g (1 lb) good-quality dark
   (bittersweet) chocolate, such as
   couverture, chopped
250 ml (9 fl oz/1 cup) milk
225 g (8 oz) unsalted butter, softened
175 g (6 oz/$^3/_4$ cup) caster (superfine)
   sugar
2 egg yolks
60 ml (2 fl oz/$^1/_4$ cup) Cointreau
   (or Grand Marnier)
24 x 4 cm (9$^1/_2$ x 1$^1/_2$ inch) blind-
   baked sweet shortcrust pastry
   case (Basics, page 177)

shaved good-quality dark
   (bittersweet) chocolate, such as
   couverture, to garnish
unsweetened cocoa powder,
   for dusting

Put the chocolate and milk in a large heavy-based saucepan over low heat, stirring occasionally, until the chocolate just melts. Remove from the heat and set aside to cool.

In the bowl of an electric mixer, cream the butter and sugar together until light and pale. Add the egg yolks, one at a time, beating well after each addition. Whisk in the cooled chocolate mixture, then whisk in the Cointreau.

Pour the chocolate filling into the blind-baked pastry case. Refrigerate for several hours, or until set.

To serve, bring the tart to room temperature (if it becomes too soft, refrigerate for about 30 minutes before serving). Arrange the shaved chocolate over the tart and dust with cocoa powder. Cut into wedges using a hot knife and serve.

Chocolate fondants with mint chocolate ice cream

Serves 6

**200 g (7 oz/1¹/₃ cups) chopped
good-quality dark (bittersweet)
chocolate, such as couverture
240 g (8¹/₂ oz) unsalted butter, diced
4 eggs
90 g (3¹/₄ oz/heaped ¹/₃ cup) caster
(superfine) sugar
30 g (1 oz) plain (all-purpose) flour**

**icing (confectioners') sugar, for
dusting
mint chocolate ice cream (page 173),
to serve**

Grease and line several baking trays with baking paper. Grease and line six 8 x 4 cm (3¹/₄ x 1¹/₂ inch) metal rings with baking paper and place them on the prepared trays; you can also use six 185 ml (6 fl oz/ ³/₄ cup) ceramic soufflé dishes that have been greased and lightly dusted with flour (shake off any excess flour).

Put the chocolate and butter in a bowl over a saucepan of simmering water and allow to melt, stirring occasionally, until smooth. Remove from the heat and allow to cool to room temperature.

In a bowl, whisk the eggs and sugar together until thick and pale. Fold in the cooled chocolate mixture, then fold in the flour. Pour into the prepared rings or soufflé dishes and refrigerate for at least 2 hours (this helps the fondants maintain their soft centre during cooking).

Preheat the oven to 200°C (400°F/Gas 6). Bake the fondants for 10–12 minutes, or until set — they should be cooked on the outside but runny in the centre.

Remove from the oven and allow to sit for a moment before turning out. If using metal rings, use a palette knife or spatula to carefully transfer the fondants to serving plates, then remove the metal ring and baking paper. Fondants cooked in soufflé dishes can be served straight from the dish.

Dust with icing sugar and serve immediately with a scoop of mint chocolate ice cream.

Sacher torte

Serves 8

225 g (8 oz/1¹/₂ cups) chopped
    good-quality dark (bittersweet)
    chocolate, such as couverture
9 eggs, separated
85 g (3 oz/¹/₃ cup) caster (superfine)
    sugar
3 teaspoons brandy
225 g (8 oz) unsalted butter, melted
1 heaped tablespoon caster
    (superfine) sugar, extra
90 g (3¹/₄ oz) plain (all-purpose) flour
3 tablespoons unsweetened cocoa
    powder
³/₄ teaspoon baking powder

CHOCOLATE GANACHE
180 g (6 oz/1¹/₂ cups) grated
    good-quality dark (bittersweet)
    chocolate, such as couverture
125 ml (4 fl oz/¹/₂ cup) pouring
    (whipping) cream

240 g (8¹/₂ oz/³/₄ cup) apricot jam,
    warmed
mixed fresh berries, to garnish
lightly whipped cream, to serve

Preheat the oven to 160°C (315°F/Gas 2–3). Grease and line the base and side of a 26 cm (10¹/2 inch) spring-form cake tin with baking paper.

Put the chopped chocolate in a heatproof bowl over a saucepan of simmering water and allow to melt, stirring occasionally, until smooth. Remove from the heat and allow to cool slightly.

In a bowl, whisk together the egg yolks, sugar and brandy until thick and pale. Add the melted butter and cooled chocolate and mix well to combine.

In the bowl of an electric mixer, whisk the egg whites until stiff peaks form, then gradually add the extra sugar and continue to whisk until all the sugar is used.

Sift together the flour, cocoa powder and baking powder, then fold into the chocolate mixture. Lastly, fold in the beaten egg whites. Pour the cake mixture into the prepared tin and bake for 50–60 minutes, or until a skewer inserted into the centre of the cake comes out clean. Allow to cool completely on a wire rack.

Meanwhile, make the chocolate ganache. Put the grated chocolate in a bowl. Bring the cream to the boil in a saucepan over high heat, then pour the cream over the chocolate, stirring until the chocolate has melted and the ganache becomes thick and glossy. Allow to cool to room temperature.

When the cake is completely cold, cut it in half horizontally. Use the top half of the cake as the base and invert onto a large serving plate. Spread with the warm apricot jam, then carefully place the remaining cake half on top. Use a palette knife or spatula to completely and evenly cover the top and sides of the torte with the chocolate ganache.

Cut into wedges and serve with fresh berries and whipped cream.

White chocolate mousse with raspberry sorbet & raspberry tuile

Serves 6

185 g (6¹/₂ oz/1¹/₄ cups) chopped good-quality white chocolate, such as couverture
2 egg whites
50 g (1³/₄ oz/¹/₄ cup) caster (superfine) sugar
375 ml (13 fl oz/1¹/₂ cups) pouring (whipping) cream, lightly whipped
1 quantity of tuile mixture (Basics, page 183)
raspberry coulis (Basics, page 183), to serve

balsamic syrup (Basics, page 176), to serve
raspberry sorbet (made using the fruit sorbet recipe on page 158), to serve
fresh raspberries, to serve

Put the chocolate in a heatproof bowl over a saucepan of simmering water and allow to melt, stirring occasionally, until smooth. Cool to room temperature.

In the bowl of an electric mixer, whisk the egg whites until soft peaks form, then gradually add the sugar and continue to whisk until all the sugar is used.

Fold the cooled chocolate into the beaten egg whites, then fold in the cream. Transfer to a glass or ceramic dish, then cover the mousse and refrigerate for several hours.

Prepare the tuile mixture as directed on page 183, adding 1 tablespoon of raspberry coulis after the flour and egg whites have been added. Refrigerate the tuile mixture for 1 hour, then continue to cook and shape as directed.

To serve, use a hot teaspoon to drizzle the balsamic syrup down one side of each serving plate, then a line of raspberry coulis across the top of the plate so they overlap. Use a large metal spoon to scoop a spoonful of white chocolate mousse into the centre. Place a tuile on top, then carefully place a spoonful of raspberry sorbet inside the tuile. Scatter the raspberries around the plate.

WARM WONDERS

The magic of food is its ability to transport us to another time and place — a warm pudding on a cold day always takes me on a journey through times past. However, these recipes needn't just be enjoyed in winter. They are appropriate for all seasons — and some are even better suited to a summer's day!

Fig tarte tatin with amaretto & mascarpone

Serves 6

22 cm (8$^1/_2$ inch) round of good-
   quality butter puff pastry
150 g (5$^1/_2$ oz/$^2/_3$ cup) caster
   (superfine) sugar
$^1/_4$ teaspoon natural vanilla extract
80 ml (2$^1/_2$ fl oz/$^1/_3$ cup) amaretto
   (almond liqueur)
12 large fresh figs, trimmed
6 amaretti biscuits (almond cookies)
250 g (9 oz/scant 1$^1/_4$ cups)
   mascarpone cheese

Grease and line a baking tray with baking paper. Lay the pastry on the prepared tray and refrigerate for 1 hour before using.

Preheat the oven to 200°C (400°F/Gas 6).

Combine the sugar and 50 ml (1$^1/_2$ fl oz) water in a small saucepan over medium heat and stir until the sugar has dissolved. Bring to the boil and boil, without stirring, until the syrup becomes a dark golden colour. Immediately remove from the heat and very carefully, as hot caramel spits, stir in the vanilla and half the amaretto. Return to the heat and stir until smooth.

Pour the caramel into a shallow 22 cm (8$^1/_2$ inch) ovenproof frying pan. Arrange the figs upside down in the caramel, fitting them snugly in the pan.

Carefully drape the rested pastry over the figs, pushing down gently at the edges. Bake for 20 minutes, or until the figs have softened and the pastry has risen and is golden in colour.

Meanwhile, lightly crush the amaretti biscuits and soak in the remaining amaretto. Once the liquid has been absorbed, stir in the mascarpone, whipping lightly if it is too soft.

Remove the tarte tatin from the oven. Pour a little of the caramel juices from the pan into a small bowl and set aside.

Place a large serving plate over the top of the pastry and carefully, as the caramel will be very hot, invert the pan to turn out the tarte tatin. Cut into wedges and place on serving plates. Top each slice with a generous spoonful of the mascarpone mixture and drizzle with the caramel juices.

The tarte tatin is best served hot, but could also be served cold.

Baked peaches with amaretti biscuit crumble

Serves 6

7 large ripe but firm peaches, cut in
  half, stones removed
12 amaretti biscuits (almond cookies),
  crushed
50 g (1³/₄ oz/¹/₂ cup) flaked almonds
60 g (2¹/₄ oz/¹/₄ cup) caster
  (superfine) sugar
100 g (3¹/₂ oz/²/₃ cup) chopped
  good-quality white chocolate,
  such as couverture
2 egg yolks
grated zest of ¹/₂ lemon
2 tablespoons amaretto (almond
  liqueur)
125 ml (4 fl oz/¹/₂ cup) light-bodied
  dessert wine
caster (superfine) sugar, for
  sprinkling
a few knobs of unsalted butter,
  diced
thick (heavy/double) cream,
  to serve

Preheat the oven to 180°C (350°F/Gas 4). Put 12 peach halves, cut side up, in a greased baking dish. Finely dice the remaining two peach halves and set aside.

Combine the biscuits, almonds, sugar and chocolate in a bowl. In a separate bowl, combine the diced peach, egg yolks, lemon zest and amaretto. Add to the dry ingredients and mix well to combine.

Fill the peach halves with the crumble mixture, then pour the dessert wine over the top. Sprinkle a little caster sugar over each peach half and dot with butter. Bake for 20–30 minutes, or until the crumble is golden.

Place two peach halves on each serving plate. Spoon the cooking juices over and serve with a spoonful of cream.

Rhubarb sponge

Serves 8

1 kg (2 lb 4 oz) rhubarb
juice of 1 orange
170 g (6 oz/$^3/_4$ cup) caster (superfine)
    sugar
1 cinnamon stick
1 vanilla bean, split lengthways,
    seeds scraped
250 g (9 oz) unsalted butter, softened
250 g (9 oz/heaped 1 cup) caster
    (superfine) sugar, extra
2 eggs
80 ml (2$^1/_2$ fl oz/$^1/_3$ cup) milk
250 g (9 oz) plain (all-purpose) flour
1 tablespoon baking powder
icing (confectioners') sugar, for
    dusting
pouring (whipping) cream, to serve

Preheat the oven to 160°C (315°F/Gas 2–3).

Trim and wash the rhubarb, cut into 5–6 cm (2–2$^1/_2$ inch) lengths, then place in a shallow baking tray. Combine the orange juice, sugar, cinnamon stick, vanilla bean and vanilla seeds, stirring until the sugar has dissolved, then pour over the rhubarb. Cover with foil and bake for 20–25 minutes, or until the rhubarb is just cooked. Set aside to cool.

Increase the oven temperature to 190°C (375°F/ Gas 5). Transfer the rhubarb to a 30 x 23 x 4 cm (12 x 9 x 1$^1/_2$ inch) baking tin with a little of the cooking syrup.

In the bowl of an electric mixer, cream the butter and extra sugar together until light and pale. Add the eggs and milk, mixing well to combine. Sift together the flour and baking powder, then fold into the creamed butter mixture. Spoon the sponge mixture over the rhubarb and bake for 45 minutes, or until the sponge springs back when touched.

Scoop large spoonfuls of the warm rhubarb sponge into serving bowls, dust with icing sugar and serve drizzled with cream.

French toast with fresh cherries & mascarpone

Serves 6

375 ml (13 fl oz/1$^{1}/_{2}$ cups) milk
6 eggs
12 slices of brioche or stale white
   bread, each about 1.5 cm ($^{5}/_{8}$ inch)
   thick, crusts on
unsalted butter, for pan-frying

220 g (7$^{3}/_{4}$ oz/1 cup) mascarpone
   cheese
600 g (1 lb 5 oz) cherries, pitted,
   stems intact
a half-quantity of cherry syrup
   (Basics, page 180), to serve
icing (confectioners') sugar,
   for dusting

In a bowl, whisk together the milk and eggs. Soak the bread in the mixture for 1–2 minutes, without allowing the bread to become too soft.

Heat a large non-stick frying pan over medium heat, add a good knob of butter and fry the bread on both sides until golden.

Place two bread slices in the centre of each serving plate and top with a good spoonful of mascarpone. Arrange a handful of cherries over the mascarpone, drizzle with the cherry syrup, dust with icing sugar and serve.

Steamed lemon pudding with crème fraîche ice cream

Serves 6

5 eggs, separated
150 g (5^1/$_2$ oz/^{2}/$_3$ cup) caster
  (superfine) sugar
50 g (1^3/$_4$ oz) unsalted butter, melted
300 ml (10^1/$_2$ fl oz) milk
3 teaspoons grated lemon zest
80 ml (2^1/$_2$ fl oz/^{1}/$_3$ cup) freshly
  squeezed lemon juice
90 g (3^1/$_4$ oz) self-raising flour, sifted
70 g (2^1/$_2$ oz/scant ^{1}/$_3$ cup) caster
  (superfine) sugar, extra

icing (confectioners') sugar, for
  dusting
crème fraîche ice cream (page 162),
  to serve

Preheat the oven to 170°C (325°F/Gas 3). Lightly grease a deep 20–24 cm (8–9^1/$_2$ inch) rectangular or round earthenware dish.

In a bowl, whisk the egg yolks and sugar together until thick and pale. Add the butter, milk, lemon zest and lemon juice, mixing well to combine. Fold in the flour.

In the bowl of an electric mixer, whisk the egg whites until stiff peaks form, then gradually add the extra sugar and continue to whisk until all the sugar is used.

Beat one-third of the beaten egg whites into the egg yolk mixture, mixing well to combine. Gently fold in the remaining beaten egg whites, then spoon into the prepared dish. Sit the baking dish in a larger roasting tin and pour in enough boiling water to come halfway up the side of the dish. Bake for 25–30 minutes, or until the pudding springs back when touched.

Place large spoonfuls of the warm pudding in serving bowls, dust with icing sugar and serve with scoops of crème fraîche ice cream.

Gingerbread puddings with prunes & Armagnac

Serves 6

180 ml (6 fl oz) boiling water

175 g (6 oz/$1/_2$ cup) golden syrup
or light corn syrup

70 g ($2^1/_2$ oz) unsalted butter,
softened

110 g ($3^3/_4$ oz/$1/_2$ cup) caster
(superfine) sugar

1 egg

150 g ($5^1/_2$ oz) plain (all-purpose)
flour

2 teaspoons baking powder

$1/_4$ teaspoon salt

1 teaspoon ground ginger

$1/_4$ teaspoon ground cinnamon

a small pinch of ground cloves

a small pinch of ground white
pepper

ARMAGNAC SAUCE

250 g (9 oz/1 heaped cup) caster
(superfine) sugar

125 ml (4 fl oz/$1/_2$ cup) Armagnac
or Cognac

125 ml (4 fl oz/$1/_2$ cup) pouring
(whipping) cream

220 g ($7^3/_4$ oz/1 cup) pitted prunes,
cut in half

lightly whipped cream,
to serve

Preheat the oven to 180°C (350°F/Gas 4). Grease six 185 ml (6 fl oz/$3/4$ cup) ramekins or dariole moulds.

Combine the boiling water and golden syrup and stir until the syrup dissolves. Set aside.

In the bowl of an electric mixer, cream the butter and sugar together until light and pale. Add the egg and mix well to combine.

Sift together the flour, baking powder, salt and ground spices. Fold the dry ingredients into the creamed butter, then add the golden syrup mixture. Beat until smooth — the mixture will be quite wet.

Pour the pudding mixture into the prepared moulds to about two-thirds full. Sit them on a baking tray and bake for 12–18 minutes, or until the puddings spring back when touched.

To make the Armagnac sauce, combine the sugar and 125 ml (4 fl oz/$1/2$ cup) water in a small saucepan over medium heat and stir until the sugar has dissolved. Bring to the boil and boil, without stirring, until the syrup becomes a dark golden colour. Immediately remove from the heat and very carefully, as hot caramel spits, stir in the Armagnac. Return to the heat and stir until smooth. Add the cream and prunes and bring just to the boil. Remove from the heat.

Turn the warm puddings out of the moulds onto serving plates. Spoon the prunes and Armagnac sauce over and serve with a spoonful of whipped cream.

Steamed quince & ginger puddings

Serves 6

160 g (5^1/$_2$ oz) unsalted butter,
  softened
160 g (5^1/$_2$ oz/scant ^{3}/$_4$ cup) caster
  (superfine) sugar
3 eggs, lightly beaten
60 ml (2 fl oz/^{1}/$_4$ cup) milk
230 g (8 oz) plain (all-purpose)
  flour
3 teaspoons baking powder
1 teaspoon ground ginger
4 poached quince quarters
  (Basics, page 181), diced
60 g (2^1/$_4$ oz/^{1}/$_4$ cup) crystallised
  ginger, roughly chopped
pouring (whipping) cream,
  to serve

Preheat the oven to 200°C (400°F/Gas 6). Lightly grease six 185 ml (6 fl oz/^{3}/$_4$ cup) ramekins or dariole moulds and line the base with a small square of baking paper.

In the bowl of an electric mixer, cream the butter and sugar together until light and pale. In a separate bowl, whisk together the eggs and milk.

Sift together the flour, baking powder, ground ginger and a pinch of salt, then fold the dry ingredients into the creamed butter, alternating with the egg mixture.

Combine the diced quince and crystallised ginger, then divide among the prepared moulds. Spoon the sponge mixture over the top to fill the moulds three-quarters full.

Loosely cover each pudding with baking paper, then cover with foil. Sit the puddings in a large roasting tin and pour in enough boiling water to come halfway up the side of the moulds. Bake for 30–40 minutes, or until the puddings spring back when touched.

Remove the puddings from the roasting tin. Run a paring knife around the edge of each mould to loosen the puddings, then turn out into the centre of serving plates. Drizzle with cream and serve.

Steamed ginger & marmalade puddings with egg custard

Serves 6

120 g (4$^{1}/_{4}$ oz) unsalted butter, softened
115 g (4 oz/$^{1}/_{2}$ cup) caster (superfine) sugar
2 eggs, lightly beaten
2 tablespoons milk
175 g (6 oz) self-raising flour, sifted
1 teaspoon ground ginger
105 g (3$^{1}/_{2}$ oz/$^{1}/_{3}$ cup) orange marmalade, roughly chopped
60 g (2$^{1}/_{4}$ oz/$^{1}/_{4}$ cup) crystallised ginger, roughly chopped

EGG CUSTARD
150 g (5$^{1}/_{2}$ oz/$^{2}/_{3}$ cup) caster (superfine) sugar
6 egg yolks
1 vanilla bean, split lengthways, seeds scraped
500 ml (17 fl oz/2 cups) pouring (whipping) cream

160 g (5$^{1}/_{2}$ oz/$^{1}/_{2}$ cup) orange marmalade, extra, thinned with 2 tablespoons boiling water

Preheat the oven to 200°C (400°F/Gas 6). Grease six 185 ml (6 fl oz/$^{3}/_{4}$ cup) ramekins or dariole moulds and line the bases with a small square of baking paper.

In the bowl of an electric mixer, cream the butter and sugar together until light and pale. In a separate bowl, whisk together the eggs and milk, then add to the creamed butter mixture and mix well.

Sift together the flour, ginger and a pinch of salt, then fold into the pudding mixture. Finally, fold in the marmalade and crystallised ginger. Spoon into the prepared moulds, loosely cover each pudding with baking paper, then cover with foil. Sit the puddings in a large roasting tin and pour in enough boiling water to come halfway up the side of the moulds. Bake for 30–40 minutes, or until the puddings spring back when touched.

Remove the puddings from the roasting tin. Run a paring knife around the edge of each mould to loosen the puddings, then turn out onto a wire rack.

Meanwhile, make the egg custard. Lightly whisk together the sugar and egg yolks. Scrape the seeds from the vanilla bean into a heavy-based saucepan. Add the vanilla bean and cream and bring almost to the boil. Remove from the heat. Whisk the hot cream mixture into the egg yolks, then return to a clean saucepan over medium heat.

Using a wooden spoon, stir constantly until the custard thickens and coats the back of the spoon. Do not let it boil. Strain through a fine sieve into a clean bowl. To stop the custard splitting, you can remove a little of the heat by placing the bowl briefly in a sink of iced water. Place a sheet of plastic wrap directly on the surface of the custard to prevent a skin forming. Keep warm.

Place the warm puddings in serving bowls and pour the custard around the puddings. Top with a small spoonful of the extra marmalade and serve.

Nectarine cobbler

Serves 6

8 large or 10 medium firm but ripe
   nectarines, cut in half, stones
   removed
caster (superfine) sugar, for dusting
220 g (7³/₄ oz) plain (all-purpose) flour
2¹/₂ teaspoons baking powder
80 g (2³/₄ oz/¹/₃ cup) caster
   (superfine) sugar, extra
60 g (2¹/₄ oz) unsalted butter,
   softened
65 g (2¹/₄ oz/³/₄ cup) flaked almonds
300 ml (10¹/₂ fl oz) pouring (whipping)
   cream, plus extra, to serve

Preheat the oven to 170°C (325°F/Gas 3). Grease a
20 cm (8 inch) ovenproof flan dish.

Lay the nectarines, cut side up, in the prepared dish.
Dust with caster sugar.

In a bowl, sift together the flour, baking powder
and a pinch of salt, then stir in the extra sugar. Rub
in the butter until the mixture resembles breadcrumbs.
Add the flaked almonds, then stir in the cream to form
a soft dough. Spoon the topping over the nectarines
and dust with a little more caster sugar. Bake for
30–35 minutes, or until the topping is golden.

Serve the cobbler warm or at room temperature,
with cream.

Cherry & almond clafoutis

Serves 6

100 g (3¹/₂ oz) plain (all-purpose)
   flour
75 g (2¹/₂ oz/¹/₃ cup) caster
   (superfine) sugar
4 eggs, separated
500 ml (17 fl oz/2 cups) milk
¹/₂ vanilla bean, split lengthways,
   seeds scraped
300 g (10¹/₂ oz) cherries, pitted,
   stems removed
raw (demerara) sugar, for sprinkling
30 g (1 oz/¹/₃ cup) flaked almonds
a few knobs of unsalted butter,
   diced
icing (confectioners') sugar,
   for dusting
vanilla bean ice cream (page 162)
   or lightly whipped cream,
   to serve

Preheat the oven to 180°C (350ºF/Gas 4). Grease a 26 cm (10¹/2 inch) ovenproof flan dish.

Sift the flour and sugar into a large bowl. In a separate bowl, whisk together the egg yolks, milk and vanilla seeds. Make a well in the centre of the dry ingredients and whisk in the egg yolk mixture.

In the bowl of an electric mixer, whisk the egg whites until stiff peaks form, then fold into the batter. Pour the batter into the prepared flan dish. Scatter the cherries over (they will sink), then sprinkle liberally with raw sugar and flaked almonds. Dot with butter and bake for 20 minutes, or until golden.

Dust with icing sugar and serve with ice cream or cream. Clafoutis is best served warm.

Peppered pineapple with vanilla bean ice cream

Serves 6

1 teaspoon whole black peppercorns
250 g (9 oz/heaped 1 cup) caster
  (superfine) sugar
80 ml (2¹/₂ fl oz/¹/₃ cup) dark rum
2 vanilla beans, split lengthways,
  seeds scraped
6 slices of pineapple, each 2 cm
  (³/₄ inch) thick

vanilla bean ice cream (page 162),
  to serve
a small handful of small mint leaves

Grind the peppercorns to a medium texture in a
mortar and pestle (a pepper mill may grind the pepper
too finely).

Combine the sugar and 100 ml (3¹/2 fl oz) water in
a small saucepan over medium heat and stir until the
sugar has dissolved. Bring to the boil and boil, without
stirring, until the syrup becomes a dark golden colour.
Immediately remove from the heat and very carefully,
as hot caramel spits, add the rum and vanilla seeds.
Add 100 ml (3¹/2 fl oz) water, return to the heat and
stir until the caramel is smooth.

Pour the caramel into a shallow frying pan. Sprinkle
both sides of each pineapple slice with the ground
pepper, then place them in the caramel. Cook over
medium heat, turning regularly, until the pineapple
is tender and golden in colour. If the caramel becomes
too thick or begins to darken, add a little more water.

Remove the pineapple slices using a spatula or
slotted spoon and place in the centre of serving plates.
Spoon the caramel over and around the pineapple, top
with a spoonful of vanilla bean ice cream and scatter
with the mint. Serve immediately.

Pear & ginger upside-down cake

Serves 6

100 g (3^1/$_2$ oz) unsalted butter,
  softened
230 g (8 oz/1^1/$_4$ cups) soft brown
  sugar
3 ripe but firm pears, unpeeled,
  cored, each cut into eight wedges
185 g (6^1/$_2$ oz) plain (all-purpose)
  flour, sifted
230 g (8 oz/1 cup) caster (superfine)
  sugar
2 teaspoons baking powder
1 teaspoon ground ginger
a good pinch of ground cinnamon
a good pinch of mixed (pumpkin pie)
  spice
2 eggs, lightly beaten
85 ml (2^3/$_4$ fl oz/^{1}/$_3$ cup) evaporated
  milk
1 teaspoon natural vanilla extract
100 g (3^1/$_2$ oz/scant ^{1}/$_2$ cup) glacé
  ginger, finely diced
120 g (4^1/$_4$ oz) unsalted butter,
  melted

230 g (8 oz/1 cup) caster (superfine)
  sugar, extra
40 g (1^1/$_2$ oz) unsalted butter,
  extra, chopped
soft ricotta cheese, to serve

Preheat the oven to 170°C (325°F/Gas 3). Grease and line the base and side of a 24 cm (9^1/2 inch) round cake tin, dust with flour and shake out any excess.

In the bowl of an electric mixer, cream the butter and brown sugar together until light and pale. Use the back of a spoon to press the mixture evenly into the base of the prepared tin. Arrange the pear wedges over the top, fanned out in a symmetrical pattern.

In a bowl, combine the flour, caster sugar, baking powder, ground spices and a pinch of salt and make a well in the centre.

In a separate bowl, whisk together the eggs, evaporated milk, vanilla, glacé ginger and 60 ml (2 fl oz/^{1}/4 cup) water until well combined. Add to the dry ingredients with the melted butter and beat to form a smooth batter.

Carefully pour the cake mixture into the tin over the pears. Bake for 1 hour, or until the cake springs back when touched. Allow to cool for 15–20 minutes in the tin before turning out.

Combine the extra caster sugar and 60 ml (2 fl oz/^{1}/4 cup) water in a small saucepan over medium heat and stir until the sugar has dissolved. Bring to the boil and boil, without stirring, until the syrup becomes a dark golden colour. Immediately remove from the heat and very carefully, as hot caramel spits, add a little cold water to stop the caramel cooking further. Return the pan to medium heat. Whisk in the butter, one piece at a time, and stir until the caramel is smooth. Remove from the heat and set aside.

Carefully invert the cake onto a cutting board and cut into wedges. Place on serving plates with a spoonful of ricotta alongside. Drizzle with the caramel and serve warm.

Date, walnut & caramel pudding

Serves 8

260 g (9¹/₄ oz/about 14–15) fresh
   dates, pitted and roughly chopped
1¹/₂ teaspoons bicarbonate of soda
   (baking soda)
90 g (3¹/₄ oz) unsalted butter,
   softened
260 g (9¹/₄ oz/scant 1¹/₄ cups) caster
   (superfine) sugar
1 teaspoon natural vanilla extract
3 eggs
260 g (9¹/₄ oz) self-raising flour
90 g (3¹/₄ oz/³/₄ cup) chopped
   walnuts
thick (double/heavy) cream,
   to serve

CARAMEL SAUCE
250 g (9 oz/1 heaped cup) caster
   (superfine) sugar
250 ml (9 fl oz/1 cup) pouring
   (whipping) cream, warmed

Preheat the oven to 180°C (350°F/Gas 4). Lightly grease a 26 cm (10¹/2 inch) ceramic or glass ovenproof dish.

Put the dates and 450 ml (16 fl oz) water in a saucepan and bring to the boil. Remove from the heat. Add the bicarbonate of soda and mix well to combine. Set aside to cool.

In the bowl of an electric mixer, cream the butter and sugar together until light and pale. Add the vanilla, then the eggs, one at a time, beating well after each addition. Add half the flour, then the date mixture and walnuts, mixing well to combine. Gradually add the remaining flour until just combined.

Spoon the pudding mixture into the prepared dish. Bake for 50–60 minutes, or until the pudding springs back when touched.

Meanwhile, make the caramel sauce. Combine the sugar and 60 ml (2 fl oz/1/4 cup) water in a small saucepan over medium heat and stir until the sugar has dissolved. Bring to the boil and boil, without stirring, until the syrup becomes a light golden colour. Immediately remove from the heat and very carefully, as hot caramel spits, stir in the cream. Return to the heat and stir until the caramel is smooth. Set aside and keep warm.

Divide the warm pudding among serving bowls using a large spoon. Pour the warm caramel sauce over and serve with a spoonful of cream.

Peach & white chocolate bread & butter pudding

Serves 6

6 eggs

250 g (9 oz/heaped 1 cup) caster (superfine) sugar

1 litre (35 fl oz/4 cups) pouring (whipping) cream

1 teaspoon natural vanilla extract

12 slices of white bread, each about 1.5 cm ($^5/_8$ inch) thick, crusts discarded

melted unsalted butter, for brushing

5 yellow peaches, stones removed, cut into wedges

150 g ($5^1/_2$ oz/1 cup) good-quality white chocolate melts (buttons)

icing (confectioners') sugar, for dusting

thick (double/heavy) cream, to serve

Preheat the oven to 140°C (275°F/Gas 1). In a large mixing bowl, whisk together the eggs, sugar, cream and vanilla. Strain the custard mixture through a fine sieve and set aside.

Preheat the oven grill (broiler) to medium. Brush both sides of each bread slice with the melted butter. Toast under the hot grill until golden, then turn and toast the other side.

Arrange the toasted bread slices in a 20–24 cm ($8–9^1/_2$ inch) rectangular or round earthenware baking dish. Pour one-third of the custard over, then top with the peach wedges and scatter with the chocolate melts. Pour over another one-third of the custard and allow to stand for 5 minutes. Pour the remaining custard over, ensuring all the bread slices are soaked in the mixture.

Sit the baking dish in a larger roasting tin and pour in enough boiling water to come halfway up the sides of the dish. Bake for 50–55 minutes, or until the custard is golden on top and set.

Use a large metal spoon to divide the warm pudding among serving plates. Dust with icing sugar and serve with a spoonful of cream.

COOL & COMPOSED

Recipes that inspire me are usually the ones that have a natural simplicity, almost to the point where you wonder if enough has been done with the dish. The recipes in this chapter aren't overly contrived or necessarily complex to make, but nor are they shy or retiring. Their superb taste, texture, clarity of flavours and aesthetic appeal make them elegantly classy.

Apple jelly & Calvados panna cotta

Makes 6–8

APPLE JELLY

1$^1/_2$ tablespoons caster (superfine) sugar

500 ml (17 fl oz/2 cups) unsweetened apple juice

$^1/_2$ tablespoon Calvados (apple liqueur) or brandy

3 gelatine leaves (6 g/$^1/_8$ oz), soaked in cold water and squeezed out

CALVADOS PANNA COTTA

100 ml (3$^1/_2$ fl oz) pouring (whipping) cream

60 ml (2 fl oz/$^1/_4$ cup) milk

2 tablespoons caster (superfine) sugar

1 tablespoon Calvados (apple liqueur) or brandy

1 gelatine leaf (2 g/$^1/_{16}$ oz), soaked in cold water and squeezed out

apple crisps (from the green apple sorbet recipe on page 156), to serve

To make the apple jelly, put the sugar and half the apple juice in a saucepan over medium heat and stir until the sugar has dissolved. Bring to the boil, then reduce the heat and simmer until reduced by half.

Add the remaining apple juice and simmer until the liquid has reduced by one-third. Whisk in the Calvados and the softened gelatine and stir to completely dissolve.

Pour the jelly mixture into six or eight shot glasses to two-thirds full. Refrigerate for several hours, or until set.

To make the Calvados panna cotta, combine the cream, milk and sugar in a small saucepan over medium heat and stir until the sugar has dissolved. Bring just to the boil, then remove from the heat. Whisk in the Calvados and softened gelatine and stir to completely dissolve. Set aside to cool.

Carefully pour the panna cotta mixture into the shot glasses over the set apple jelly. Refrigerate for several hours, or until set.

Apple jellies can be served as a dessert taster with apple crisps, or to accompany an apple dessert such as a slice of apple tart, apple strudel or a whole baked apple.

Passionfruit ice cream & sesame wafer sandwich

Serves 6

**1 quantity of passionfruit ice cream
  (page 163)**
6 passionfruit, cut in half
**1–2 teaspoons icing (confectioners')
  sugar**

18 sesame wafers (Basics, page 184)
**icing (confectioners') sugar, for
  dusting, optional**

Prepare the passionfruit ice cream as directed. Once fully churned, spoon the ice cream into a shallow tray to a depth of 1 cm ($^1/_2$ inch), then freeze.

Scoop the pulp and seeds from the passionfruit into a food processor. Stir in some icing sugar to taste. Using the pulse button, process briefly to loosen the seeds from the pulp. Strain the liquid from the seeds and add a few seeds back into the passionfruit syrup for colour.

Use an 8 cm ($3^1/_4$ inch) pastry cutter to stamp out the ice cream into 12 discs. Place a sesame wafer on each serving plate, then top with a disc of ice cream. Repeat the layering, finishing with a third wafer on top. Drizzle the passionfruit syrup around the plate and dust with icing sugar if desired.

Honey parfait with grilled plums & pistachios

Serves 8

250 ml (9 fl oz/1 cup) milk
90 g (3¼ oz/¼ cup) good-quality
  honey
1 vanilla bean, split lengthways,
  seeds scraped
6 egg yolks
115 g (4 oz/½ cup) caster (superfine)
  sugar
350 ml (12 fl oz) pouring (whipping)
  cream
10 ripe but firm plums, cut in half,
  stones removed

caster (superfine) sugar, for
  sprinkling
40 g (1½ oz/¼ cup) shelled,
  unsalted pistachio nuts, blanched
  and skinned

Put the milk, honey, vanilla bean and vanilla seeds in a saucepan over medium heat and stir to dissolve the honey. Bring to the boil, then remove from the heat.

In a bowl, lightly whisk together the egg yolks and sugar. Whisk in the hot milk mixture, then return to a clean saucepan over medium heat.

Using a wooden spoon, stir constantly until the custard thickens and coats the back of the spoon. Do not allow to boil. Strain through a fine sieve into the bowl of an electric mixer. Beat on medium speed until cool, then refrigerate until completely cold.

Whisk the cream until stiff peaks form. Using a whisk, carefully fold the cream through the custard mixture, a little at a time, so that you don't lose any volume.

Line a 28 x 10 x 8 cm (11¼ x 4 x 3¼ inch) rectangular loaf (bar) tin with plastic wrap, allowing a 4 cm (1½ inch) overhang around the sides. Spoon the parfait mixture into the tin, then tap the tin lightly on a work surface to remove air bubbles. Gently cover the top with the overhanging plastic wrap and freeze overnight, or until set.

Preheat the oven grill (broiler) to medium. Sprinkle the cut surface of each plum half liberally with caster sugar and place on a baking tray. Grill for 6–8 minutes, or until the plums caramelise on top.

Turn the parfait out of the mould onto a cutting board. Using a hot knife, cut it into slices about 1.5 cm (⁵/8 inch) thick, then arrange two slices in the centre of each serving plate. Arrange the plum halves over the parfait and drizzle with a little of the cooking juices. Scatter with pistachio nuts.

Praline semi-freddo with fresh raspberries

Serves 8

100 g (3^1/$_2$ oz/scant ^{1}/$_2$ cup) caster
  (superfine) sugar
100 g (3^1/$_2$ oz/^{2}/$_3$ cup) hazelnuts,
  roasted and skinned
185 g (6^1/$_2$ oz/heaped ^{3}/$_4$ cup) caster
  (superfine) sugar, extra
5 egg whites
280 ml (9^1/$_2$ fl oz) pouring (whipping)
  cream, lightly whipped
50 ml (1^1/$_2$ fl oz) Frangelico (hazelnut
  liqueur)

raspberry coulis (Basics, page 183),
  to serve
fresh raspberries, to serve

Grease and line a baking tray with baking paper.

Put the sugar and just enough water to cover in a heavy-based saucepan over medium heat and stir until the sugar has dissolved. Bring to the boil and boil, without stirring, until the syrup becomes a dark golden colour. Immediately remove from the heat and add all the hazelnuts at once. Quickly pour the mixture over the prepared tray and flatten out using the back of a hot metal spoon. Allow to cool. Once cold, break the praline into small pieces in a mortar and pestle, or break up in a food processor, using the pulse button. Set aside, reserving 2 tablespoons of the praline to garnish.

Combine the extra sugar and 100 ml (3^1/2 fl oz) water in a heavy-based saucepan over medium heat and stir until the sugar has dissolved. Bring to the boil, then reduce the heat and simmer, stirring constantly, for 15–20 minutes, or until the temperature reaches 120°C (248°F) on a sugar thermometer, or the mixture reaches the soft-ball stage.

Meanwhile, whisk the egg whites in the bowl of an electric mixer until stiff peaks form. When the sugar syrup reaches 120°C (248°F), gradually add it to the beaten egg whites in a constant steady stream, whisking constantly until cold. Use a whisk to carefully fold in the cream, Frangelico and praline.

Line a 28 x 10 x 8 cm (11^1/4 x 4 x 3^1/4 inch) rectangular loaf (bar) tin with plastic wrap, allowing a 4 cm (1^1/2 inch) overhang around the sides.

Spoon the semi-freddo mixture into the mould, then tap the tin lightly on a work surface to remove air bubbles. Gently cover the top with the overhanging plastic wrap and freeze overnight, or until set.

Turn the semi-freddo out of the mould onto a cutting board. Using a hot knife, cut it into slices about 1.5 cm (^{5}/8 inch) thick and arrange two slices in the centre of each serving plate. Sprinkle with the reserved praline. Drizzle the raspberry coulis around the plate and scatter with raspberries.

Saffron crema catalana

Serves 6

1 litre (35 fl oz/4 cups) thick (double/
   heavy) cream
1 vanilla bean, split lengthways,
   seeds scraped
a good pinch of saffron threads,
   infused in 1 tablespoon of boiling
   water
1 cinnamon stick
zest of 1 orange, peeled into strips
12 egg yolks
130 g (4$^{1}/_{2}$ oz/scant $^{2}/_{3}$ cup) caster
   (superfine) sugar

caster (superfine) sugar, for sprinkling
a half-quantity of biscotti (Basics,
   page 176), to serve

Put the cream, vanilla bean, vanilla seeds, saffron-infused water, cinnamon stick and orange zest in a large saucepan and bring to the boil. Remove from the heat and set aside to infuse for 15 minutes.

Strain the cream through a fine sieve. Return to a clean saucepan and bring back to the boil, then remove from the heat.

In a large bowl, lightly whisk together the egg yolks and sugar. Whisk in the hot cream mixture, then return to a clean saucepan over medium heat.

Using a wooden spoon, stir constantly until the custard thickens and coats the back of the spoon. Do not let it boil. Strain through a fine sieve, then pour into six shallow 10 cm (4 inch) round or square serving dishes. Refrigerate until set, preferably overnight.

To serve, sprinkle each crema catalana liberally with caster sugar. Using a kitchen blowtorch, or under a very hot oven grill (broiler), caramelise the sugar. Serve with biscotti.

Cheat's strawberry trifle

Serves 8

1 small, plain ready-made sponge
 cake (about 150 g/5^1/$_2$ oz)
200 ml (7 fl oz) sweet sherry
85 g (3 oz) packet strawberry jelly
 (gelatine dessert) crystals
500 ml (17 fl oz/2 cups) milk
3 tablespoons custard powder
 (instant vanilla pudding mix)
70 g (2^1/$_2$ oz/scant ^{1}/$_3$ cup) caster
 (superfine) sugar

500 g (1 lb 2 oz) strawberries,
 hulled and halved
500 ml (17 fl oz/2 cups) pouring
 (whipping) cream, lightly
 whipped
155 g (5^1/$_2$ oz/1 cup) whole blanched
 almonds, roasted and roughly
 chopped

Cut the sponge cake into 2 cm (^{3}/$_4$ inch) squares and place in a glass bowl that is about 20–25 cm (8–10 inch) deep. Pour the sherry over. Prepare the jelly according to the packet instructions, then pour over the sponge. Cover and refrigerate, preferably overnight, for the jelly to set.

Mix 60 ml (2 fl oz/^{1}/$_4$ cup) of the milk with the custard powder to form a smooth paste.

Put the remaining milk and sugar in a heavy-based saucepan over medium heat and stir until the sugar has dissolved. Bring to the boil, then drizzle in the custard mixture, whisking constantly to prevent lumps forming. Reduce the heat to a simmer and cook for 2–3 minutes, stirring occasionally. Remove from the heat and set aside to cool slightly. Pour the custard over the set jelly and refrigerate until cool.

To serve, arrange the strawberries over the custard. Spread the whipped cream over the strawberries and scatter with the almonds.

Trifle is best eaten on the day it is made.

Mandarin creams

Serves 6

185 ml (6 fl oz/$^3/_4$ cup) freshly
squeezed mandarin juice,
strained
450 ml (16 fl oz) pouring (whipping)
cream
115 g (4 oz/$^1/_2$ cup) caster (superfine)
sugar
1 tablespoon freshly squeezed
lemon juice

3 mandarins, peeled, segmented,
seeded and chopped
a small handful of mint leaves,
shredded
Cointreau, optional, for drizzling

Put the mandarin juice in a small saucepan over medium heat. Bring to the boil and simmer until reduced by two-thirds.

In a large saucepan, heat the cream. When it is hot but not boiling, stir in the sugar, then bring to the boil and boil for 3 minutes.

Remove from the heat, then stir in the lemon juice and reduced mandarin juice. Strain through a fine sieve into a pouring jug, then divide evenly among martini-style serving glasses. Refrigerate until set, preferably overnight.

To serve, pile a little chopped mandarin on top of each mandarin cream and scatter with the mint. Drizzle with a little Cointreau, if desired.

NOTE: These mandarin creams could also be served in 12 shot glasses as a dessert taster or to accompany a citrus tart.

Spiced pears with labneh & pistachios

Serves 6

LABNEH
400 g (14 oz) Greek-style yoghurt
30 g (1 oz/^{1}/$_4$ cup) icing
**   (confectioners') sugar**
a pinch of ground cinnamon

SPICED PEARS
600 g (1 lb 5 oz/2^2/$_3$ cups) caster
**   (superfine) sugar**
4 cardamom pods, roasted, crushed
**   and sieved**
1 cinnamon stick
3 star anise
zest of 1 lemon
2 vanilla beans, split lengthways,
**   seeds scraped**
6 large or 9 small ripe but firm pears,
**   peeled, cut in half and cored**

75 g (2^1/$_2$ oz/^{1}/$_2$ cup) shelled,
**   unsalted pistachio nuts, blanched**
**   and skinned**

To make the labneh, combine the yoghurt, icing sugar and cinnamon in a bowl. Sit a strainer inside a large bowl and line with a large piece of muslin (cheesecloth), leaving a good overhang. Spoon the yoghurt into the centre, cover with the overhanging muslin, then refrigerate for 24 hours to allow any excess moisture to drain and for the yoghurt to become firm.

To make the spiced pears, combine the sugar and 800 ml (28 fl oz) water in a large heavy-based saucepan over medium heat and stir until the sugar has dissolved. Add the cardamom, cinnamon stick, star anise, lemon zest, vanilla beans and vanilla seeds. Bring to the boil, then reduce the heat and simmer for 5 minutes. Reduce the heat to low, add the pears, then cover with baking paper and a plate to keep them completely submerged. Poach gently for 12–15 minutes, or until tender. Using a slotted spoon, transfer the pears to a bowl, then pour half the poaching liquid over. Set aside to cool.

Strain the remaining poaching liquid through a fine sieve and return to a clean saucepan over medium heat, discarding the aromatics. Bring to the boil, then reduce the heat and simmer until reduced by one-third. Set aside until required.

Arrange two or three pear halves in the centre of serving bowls, with a spoonful of labneh alongside. Drizzle a little of the reduced poaching liquid over and around the pears and scatter with the pistachios. Serve cold, or at room temperature.

Lychee mousse with pineapple & passionfruit

Serves 6

450 g (1 lb/2 cups) caster (superfine) sugar

80 g (2³/₄ oz/¹/₃ cup) glucose syrup

1 kg (2 lb 4 oz) fresh lychees, peeled and seeded, or 550 g (1 lb 4 oz) drained tinned lychees

7 gelatine leaves (14 g/¹/₂ oz), soaked in cold water and squeezed out

2 egg whites

460 ml (16 fl oz) pouring (whipping) cream, lightly whipped

¹/₂ pineapple, core removed, finely diced

1 makrut (kaffir lime) leaf, finely sliced

3 passionfruit, cut in half

Combine the sugar, glucose syrup and 400 ml (14 fl oz) water in a heavy-based saucepan over medium heat and stir until the sugar has dissolved. Bring to the boil, then remove from the heat and allow the sugar syrup to cool.

Purée the lychees in a food processor until smooth, then transfer to a large mixing bowl. Gently heat a small amount of the lychee purée in a non-stick saucepan. Whisk in the softened gelatine and stir to completely dissolve, then mix into the lychee purée.

Measure 125 ml (4 fl oz/¹/₂ cup) of the sugar syrup into a small saucepan over medium heat. Bring to the boil, then reduce the heat and simmer, stirring constantly, for about 5 minutes, or until the temperature reaches 120°C (248°F) on a sugar thermometer, or the mixture reaches the soft-ball stage.

Meanwhile, whisk the egg whites in the bowl of an electric mixer until stiff peaks form. When the sugar syrup reaches 120°C (248°F), gradually add it to the beaten egg whites in a constant steady stream, whisking constantly until cold.

Gradually fold the beaten egg whites into the lychee purée, incorporating it well, then fold in the cream. Divide among six 250–300 ml (9–10¹/₂ fl oz) serving glasses or moulds and refrigerate for at least 5 hours to set.

To serve, combine the pineapple, lime leaf and pulp from the passionfruit and spoon over each lychee mousse.

Cherries poached in Valpolicella with yoghurt gelato

Serves 6

zest of 1 lemon, peeled into strips
1 cinnamon stick
2 vanilla beans, split lengthways,
    seeds scraped
200 g (7 oz/scant 1 cup) caster
    (superfine) sugar
750 ml (26 fl oz/3 cups) Valpolicella,
    or similar light-bodied, fruity Italian
    red wine
1.2 kg (2 lb 11 oz) cherries, pitted,
    stems intact

yoghurt gelato (page 159), to serve
grated zest of 1 lime

Combine the lemon zest, cinnamon stick, vanilla beans, vanilla seeds, sugar, wine and 600 ml (21 fl oz) water in a saucepan over medium heat and stir until the sugar has dissolved. Bring to the boil, then reduce the heat to a simmer.

Add the cherries and cover with a sheet of baking paper. Poach gently for 3–5 minutes, depending on the size of the cherries, being careful not to overcook them or they will lose their colour. Remove from the heat and allow to cool in the poaching liquid. Remove the cherries using a slotted spoon and place in a bowl.

Return the poaching liquid to medium heat, bring to the boil, then reduce the heat and simmer until reduced by two-thirds. Remove from the heat and set aside to cool.

Pour the cooled syrup over the cherries and refrigerate until required.

To serve, spoon the poached cherries into serving bowls with a little of the poaching liquid. Add a spoonful of yoghurt gelato and sprinkle with the lime zest.

Pears poached in red wine with pain d'épices

Serves 6

zest of 1 lemon, peeled into strips
1 cinnamon stick
200 g (7 oz/scant 1 cup) caster
  (superfine) sugar
750 ml (26 fl oz/3 cups) light-bodied,
  fruity Italian red wine
6 ripe but firm pears, peeled, halved
  and cored

PAIN D'EPICES
100 g (3$^1/_2$ oz) unsalted butter,
  softened
250 g (9 oz/1$^1/_3$ cups) soft brown
  sugar
3 eggs
220 g (7$^3/_4$ oz) plain (all-purpose)
  flour
2 tablespoons ground almonds
1 tablespoon baking powder
1 teaspoon ground cinnamon
$^1/_4$ teaspoon ground cardamom
$^1/_2$ teaspoon ground cloves
grated zest of $^1/_2$ orange
2 teaspoons finely chopped
  crystallised ginger
200 ml (7 fl oz) milk
juice of 1 orange
2 tablespoons orange marmalade,
  chopped

icing (confectioners') sugar, for
  dusting
mascarpone cheese or lightly
  whipped cream, to serve

Combine the lemon zest, cinnamon stick, sugar, wine and 600 ml (21 fl oz) water in a large saucepan over medium heat and stir until the sugar has dissolved. Bring to the boil, then reduce to a simmer. Immerse the pears and cover with baking paper and a plate to keep them submerged. Poach for 12–15 minutes, or until tender.

Allow the pears to cool in the poaching liquid, then transfer to a bowl and set aside. Strain the poaching liquid through a fine sieve and return to a clean saucepan, discarding the aromatics. Return the pan to medium heat and simmer until reduced by one-third. Pour the reduced syrup over the pears and refrigerate until required.

Preheat the oven to 160°C (315°F/Gas 2–3). Grease and line the base and sides of a shallow 30 x 23 x 4 cm (12 x 9 x 1$^1/_2$ inch) baking tin with baking paper.

To make the pain d'épices, cream the butter and sugar together in the bowl of an electric mixer until light and pale. Add the eggs, one at a time, beating well after each addition.

In a separate bowl, combine the flour, almonds, baking powder, ground spices, orange zest and ginger, then fold into the creamed butter mixture. Add the milk, orange juice and marmalade, mixing well. Pour the mixture into the prepared tin and bake for 50–60 minutes, or until the cake pulls away from the side of the tin. Allow to cool in the tin before turning out.

Use a slotted spoon to remove the pears from the poaching syrup; set aside. Heat the syrup in a saucepan over medium heat, bring to the boil, then remove from the heat.

Cut the pain d'épices into 7 cm (2^3/4 inch) squares, dust liberally with icing sugar and place in the centre of serving plates. Arrange two pear halves on top, drizzle with the warm syrup and serve with a spoonful of mascarpone or whipped cream. Leftover pain d'épices will keep for two days stored in an airtight container.

Honey Bavarian cream with balsamic strawberries

Serves 6

8 egg yolks
2 tablespoons honey
115 g (4 oz/$\frac{1}{2}$ cup) caster (superfine)
  sugar
1 vanilla bean, split lengthways
250 ml (9 fl oz/1 cup) milk
250 ml (9 fl oz/1 cup) pouring
  (whipping) cream
4 gelatine leaves (8 g/$\frac{1}{6}$ oz), soaked
  in cold water and squeezed out
250 ml (9 fl oz/1 cup) pouring
  (whipping) cream, extra, lightly
  whipped

BALSAMIC STRAWBERRIES
50 g (1$\frac{3}{4}$ oz/$\frac{1}{4}$ cup) caster
  (superfine) sugar
90 ml (3 fl oz) Cointreau
3 teaspoons good-quality balsamic
  vinegar
500 g (1 lb 2 oz) strawberries,
  hulled and halved

a small handful of mint leaves,
  finely sliced

In a bowl, lightly whisk together the egg yolks, honey and half the sugar.

Scrape the seeds from the vanilla bean into a heavy-based saucepan. Add the vanilla bean, milk, cream and remaining sugar and bring almost to the boil. Remove from the heat.

Whisk the hot milk mixture into the egg yolk mixture, then return to a clean saucepan over medium heat.

Using a wooden spoon, stir constantly until the custard thickens and coats the back of the spoon. Do not let it boil. Strain through a fine sieve, then measure out 500 ml (17 fl oz/2 cups) of the custard and place in a bowl.

Rinse six 125 ml (4 fl oz/$\frac{1}{2}$ cup) plastic dariole moulds with cold water.

Whisk the softened gelatine into the hot custard, then sit the bowl over iced water to cool, stirring constantly to stop it setting. Once cold, fold in the whipped cream, then immediately pour into the prepared moulds. Refrigerate until set, preferably overnight.

To make the balsamic strawberries, combine the sugar, Cointreau and vinegar in a small saucepan over low heat and stir until the sugar has dissolved. Carefully tilt the pan and use a match to ignite and burn off the alcohol. Once the flame goes out, remove from the heat and allow to cool to room temperature. Pour over the strawberries and set aside for 15 minutes to macerate.

To serve, run a warm paring knife around the edge of each mould to loosen the Bavarian creams, then invert and gently squeeze into the centre of serving bowls. Spoon the balsamic strawberries around the bowl and scatter with the mint.

Mandarin jelly bavarois

Serves 8

MANDARIN JELLY
300 ml (10^1/$_2$ fl oz) freshly squeezed mandarin juice, strained
3 gelatine leaves (6 g/^{1}/$_8$ oz), soaked in cold water and squeezed out
50 g (1^3/$_4$ oz/^{1}/$_4$ cup) caster (superfine) sugar

BAVAROIS
3 egg yolks
75 g (2^1/$_2$ oz/^{1}/$_3$ cup) caster (superfine) sugar
250 ml (9 fl oz/1 cup) milk
1 vanilla bean, split lengthways, seeds scraped
2 gelatine leaves (4 g/^{1}/$_8$ oz), soaked in cold water and squeezed out
250 ml (9 fl oz/1 cup) pouring (whipping) cream, lightly whipped

MANDARIN SYRUP
250 g (9 oz/heaped 1 cup) caster (superfine) sugar
125 ml (4 fl oz/^{1}/$_2$ cup) freshly squeezed mandarin juice, strained

mandarin segments, to serve
a half-quantity of biscotti (Basics, page 176), to serve
icing (confectioners') sugar, for dusting

To make the mandarin jelly, heat 100 ml (3^1/2 fl oz) of the mandarin juice in a small saucepan over low heat. Remove from the heat, whisk in the softened gelatine and stir to completely dissolve. Return to low heat. Add the sugar and remaining mandarin juice and stir until the sugar has dissolved. Remove from the heat.

Rinse eight 125 ml (4 fl oz/1/2 cup) plastic dariole moulds with cold water. Pour the jelly into the moulds to a depth of about 1 cm (1/2 inch). Set aside (do not refrigerate).

Meanwhile, to make the bavarois, lightly whisk together the egg yolks and sugar in a bowl. Put the milk, vanilla bean and vanilla seeds in a heavy-based saucepan over medium heat and bring almost to the boil. Whisk the hot milk mixture into the egg yolks, then return to a clean saucepan over medium heat.

Using a wooden spoon, stir constantly until the custard thickens and coats the back of the spoon. Do not let it boil. Remove from the heat, whisk in the softened gelatine and stir to completely dissolve. Strain through a fine sieve into a bowl, then set aside and allow to cool to room temperature, stirring occasionally — the mixture will start to thicken. Just as the mixture is almost set, fold in the whipped cream.

Divide the bavarois mixture among the moulds when the jelly is nearly set — this will help make it stick to the jelly, otherwise it may come out in two parts. Refrigerate until set, preferably overnight.

To make the mandarin syrup, combine the sugar and 60 ml (2 fl oz/1/4 cup) water in a small saucepan over medium heat and stir until the sugar has dissolved. Bring to the boil and boil, without stirring, until the syrup becomes a dark golden colour. Immediately remove from the heat and very carefully, as hot caramel spits, add the mandarin juice. Return to low heat and stir until smooth. Set aside to cool.

To serve, run a warm paring knife around the edge of each mould to loosen the bavarois, then invert and gently squeeze into the centre of serving bowls. Drizzle the mandarin syrup around the bavarois and scatter with mandarin segments. Serve with biscotti, dusted with icing sugar.

Little citrus creams

Makes 12 shot glasses

450 ml (16 fl oz) pouring (whipping)
   cream
115 g (4 oz/$1/2$ cup) caster (superfine)
   sugar
75 ml ($2^1/_4$ fl oz) freshly squeezed
   lemon juice

1 lemon
fresh raspberries, to serve

Arrange twelve 45 ml ($1^1/2$ fl oz) shot glasses on
a tray.

Put the cream and sugar in a large saucepan over
medium heat and stir until the sugar has dissolved.
Bring to the boil and boil for 3 minutes. Remove from
the heat, then stir in the lemon juice.

Strain through a fine sieve into a pouring jug.
Divide evenly among the shot glasses so that each
glass is about three-quarters full. Refrigerate until
set, preferably overnight.

Peel the zest from the lemon into wide strips using
a vegetable peeler, then use a sharp knife to remove
any white pith from the zest. Blanch the lemon zest
in a small saucepan of boiling water for 2 minutes.
Refresh in iced water. Blanch the zest for a further
2 minutes, refresh in iced water once again, then cut
into thin strips.

Serve the citrus creams topped with the lemon zest
and raspberries.

NOTE: These little citrus creams can be served as a
dessert taster or to accompany a citrus tart. You could
also serve them as a full-sized dessert in six martini
glasses with biscotti (see Basics, page 176).

Vanilla creamed rice with cinnamon-spiced apples

Serves 6

60 g (2$^1/_4$ oz) unsalted butter

90 g (3$^1/_4$ oz/heaped $^1/_3$ cup) caster (superfine) sugar

125 g (4$^1/_2$ oz/$^2/_3$ cup) short- or medium-grain rice

1 vanilla bean, split lengthways, seeds scraped

500 ml (17 fl oz/2 cups) milk

500 ml (17 fl oz/2 cups) pouring (whipping) cream

CINNAMON-SPICED APPLES

50 g (1$^3/_4$ oz) unsalted butter

6 granny smith apples, peeled, cored and each cut into 8 wedges

2 tablespoons caster (superfine) sugar

60 g (2$^1/_4$ oz/$^1/_2$ cup) raisins

$^1/_2$ teaspoon ground cinnamon

Preheat the oven to 160°C (315°F/Gas 2–3). Melt the butter in a heavy-based saucepan over low heat, then add the sugar and rice. Stir for 5 minutes. Add the vanilla bean, vanilla seeds, milk, cream and a pinch of salt and bring to the boil.

Pour the mixture into a shallow baking dish and cover with foil. Sit the dish in a larger roasting tin and pour in enough warm water to come halfway up the side of the dish. Bake for 60–80 minutes, stirring every 20 minutes, until the rice is soft and creamy. The mixture will appear fairly wet, but the rice will absorb this liquid as it cools. Remove the dish from the oven and stir occasionally while cooling. Refrigerate until required.

To make the cinnamon-spiced apples, melt the butter in a large, heavy-based frying pan over medium–high heat. Add the apple wedges and quickly sauté on all sides until they soften slightly. Add the sugar, raisins and cinnamon and continue to cook, allowing any liquid to evaporate. Spread the apple wedges onto a tray to cool.

To serve, place a large spoonful of creamed rice into serving glasses or bowls. The apples can be served at room temperature, or gently reheated and spooned over the rice.

NOTE: Creamed rice is best served at room temperature on the day it is made. It could be made in advance and refrigerated, although it may be too firm served straight from the fridge. Prior to serving, fold in a little milk or cream if necessary.

Iced passionfruit parfait

Serves 10

4 eggs, separated
300 g (10^1/$_2$ oz/1^1/$_3$ cups) caster
    (superfine) sugar
250 ml (9 fl oz/1 cup) milk
250 ml (9 fl oz/1 cup) passionfruit
    pulp (see Note)
250 ml (9 fl oz/1 cup) pouring
    (whipping) cream, lightly whipped

3 passionfruit, cut in half
caramel shards (Basics, page 178),
    to serve

In a bowl, lightly whisk together the egg yolks and 170 g (6 oz/^{3}/$_4$ cup) of the sugar.

Heat the milk in a small saucepan and bring almost to the boil. Whisk the hot milk into the egg yolks, then return to a clean saucepan over medium heat.

Using a wooden spoon, stir constantly until the custard thickens and coats the back of the spoon. Do not let it boil. Strain through a fine sieve, then refrigerate until cold. Once cold, stir in the passionfruit pulp.

Combine the remaining sugar and 100 ml (3^1/$_2$ fl oz) water in a small saucepan over medium heat and stir until the sugar has dissolved. Bring to the boil, then reduce the heat and simmer, stirring constantly, for 5 minutes, or until the temperature reaches 120°C (248°F) on a sugar thermometer, or the mixture reaches the soft-ball stage.

Meanwhile, whisk the egg whites in the bowl of an electric mixer until stiff peaks form. When the sugar syrup reaches 120°C (248°F), gradually add it to the beaten egg whites in a constant steady stream, whisking constantly until cold. Fold in the cream then, using a rubber spatula or whisk, very carefully fold in the passionfruit mixture.

Line a 30 x 12 x 10 cm (12 x 4^1/$_2$ x 4 inch) triangular terrine mould or rectangular loaf (bar) tin with plastic wrap, allowing a 4 cm (1^1/$_2$ inch) overhang around the sides. Pour the mixture into the mould, then tap the tin lightly on a work surface to remove air bubbles. Gently cover the top with the overhanging plastic wrap and freeze overnight, or until set.

Turn the parfait out of the mould onto a cutting board. Using a hot knife, cut it into slices about 1.5 cm (^{5}/$_8$ inch) thick and arrange two slices in the centre of each serving plate. Spoon the pulp from the passionfruit around the plate and top with caramel shards.

NOTE: Fresh passionfruit pulp is preferable for this recipe, although it is sometimes also available frozen.

Iced banana & rum parfait

Serves 10

3 bananas
juice of 1 lemon
45 ml (1$^1/_2$ fl oz) dark rum
230 g (8 oz/1 cup) caster (superfine)
    sugar
5 egg yolks
3 egg whites
300 ml (10$^1/_2$ fl oz) pouring
    (whipping) cream, lightly whipped

PRALINE
250 g (9 oz/heaped 1 cup) caster
    (superfine) sugar
150 g (5$^1/_2$ oz/heaped 1 cup)
    hazelnuts, roasted and skinned

ORANGE CARAMEL
250 g (9 oz/heaped 1 cup) caster
    (superfine) sugar
100 ml (3$^1/_2$ fl oz) freshly squeezed
    orange juice

1 quantity of sesame wafers
    (Basics, page 184), made using an
    8 cm (3$^1/_4$ inch) triangle stencil

Put the bananas, lemon juice and rum in a food processor and blend until smooth. Set aside.

Place 150 g (5$^1/_2$ oz/$^2/_3$ cup) of the sugar and 125 ml (4 fl oz/$^1/_2$ cup) water in a small heavy-based saucepan over medium heat and stir until the sugar has dissolved. Bring to the boil, then reduce the heat and simmer until the sugar syrup just begins to change colour.

Meanwhile, whisk the egg yolks in the bowl of an electric mixer. As the sugar syrup begins to change colour, gradually add it to the egg yolks in a constant steady stream, whisking constantly until cold.

In a separate bowl, whisk the egg whites until stiff peaks form, then gradually add the remaining sugar and continue to whisk until all the sugar is used.

Fold the cream into the egg yolk mixture, then fold in the banana purée. Lastly, fold in the beaten egg whites.

Line a 30 x 12 x 10 cm (12 x 4$^1/_2$ x 4 inch) triangular terrine mould or rectangular loaf (bar) tin with plastic wrap, allowing a 4 cm (1$^1/_2$ inch) overhang around the sides. Pour the mixture into the mould, then tap lightly on a work surface to remove air bubbles. Gently cover the top with the overhanging plastic wrap and freeze overnight, or until set.

To make the praline, grease and line a baking tray with baking paper. Put the sugar and just enough water to cover in a heavy-based saucepan over medium heat and stir until the sugar has dissolved. Bring to the boil and boil, without stirring, until the syrup becomes a dark golden colour. Immediately remove from the heat and add all the hazelnuts at once. Quickly pour the mixture over the prepared tray and flatten out with the back of a hot metal spoon. Allow to cool. Once cold, break into small pieces in a mortar and pestle, or break up in a food processor, using the pulse button.

To make the orange caramel, combine the sugar and 100 ml (3$^1/_2$ fl oz) water in a saucepan over medium heat and stir until the sugar has dissolved. Bring to the boil and boil, without stirring, until the syrup becomes a dark golden colour. Immediately remove from the heat and very carefully, as hot caramel spits, stir in the orange juice. Return the pan to low heat and stir until smooth. Remove from the heat and set aside to cool.

Turn the parfait out of the mould onto a cutting board. Using a hot knife, cut it into slices about 1.5 cm ($^5/_8$ inch) thick and arrange two slices in the centre of each serving plate. Spoon the orange caramel over the parfait, sprinkle with the praline and serve with sesame wafers.

Eton mess

Serves 6

3 egg whites

175 g (6 oz/³/₄ cup) caster (superfine) sugar

500 g (1 lb 2 oz) strawberries, hulled and halved

1 tablespoon icing (confectioners') sugar

600 ml (21 fl oz) pouring (whipping) cream, lightly whipped

Preheat the oven to 150°C (300°F/Gas 2). Grease and line a baking tray with baking paper.

In the bowl of an electric mixer, whisk the egg whites until soft peaks form, then gradually add the sugar and continue to whisk until all the sugar is used. Spread the meringue mixture on the prepared tray to an even 1 cm (1/2 inch) thickness and bake for 40 minutes. Turn the oven off and allow to dry in the oven for about 1 hour.

Meanwhile, place half the strawberries and the icing sugar in a food processor or blender and purée until smooth. Strain the purée through a fine sieve or piece of muslin (cheesecloth) to remove the seeds. Set aside.

Break the meringue into small pieces and place in a large mixing bowl with the remaining strawberries. Fold in the whipped cream. Lastly, fold in a little of the strawberry purée to create a marbled effect — do not overmix.

Divide among six individual serving glasses or spoon into a large glass bowl. Drizzle with the remaining strawberry purée and serve immediately.

Espresso & Cognac mousse with shortbread

Serves 6

3 gelatine leaves (6 g/$^1/_8$ oz), soaked
 in cold water and squeezed out
125 ml (4 fl oz/$^1/_2$ cup) hot espresso
 or strong plunger coffee
330 ml (11$^1/_4$ fl oz/1$^1/_3$ cups)
 pouring (whipping) cream, lightly
 whipped
1 teaspoon natural vanilla extract
2 eggs
70 g (2$^1/_2$ oz/scant $^1/_3$ cup) caster
 (superfine) sugar
1 tablespoon Cognac or brandy

SHORTBREAD
125 g (4$^1/_2$ oz) unsalted butter,
 softened
80 g (2$^3/_4$ oz/$^1/_3$ cup) caster
 (superfine) sugar
1 teaspoon natural vanilla extract
1 teaspoon grated lemon zest
1 tablespoon rice flour
115 g (4 oz) plain (all-purpose) flour
1 tablespoon caster (superfine)
 sugar, extra

lightly whipped cream, to serve
unsweetened cocoa powder,
 for dusting

In a small bowl, whisk the softened gelatine into the hot coffee and stir to completely dissolve. Set aside.

In a bowl, whisk the cream and vanilla to soft peaks. In a separate bowl, whisk together the eggs, sugar and Cognac until thick and pale. Stir in the warm coffee mixture, then use a whisk to carefully fold in the whipped cream. Divide among six coffee cups or small serving glasses and refrigerate until set, preferably overnight.

Preheat the oven to 160°C (315°F/Gas 2–3). Grease and line the base and side of a 26 cm (10^1/2 inch) spring-form cake tin with baking paper.

To make the shortbread, cream the butter and sugar together in the bowl of an electric mixer until light and pale. Add the vanilla and lemon zest. Sift together the rice flour and flour, then fold into the creamed butter mixture. On a floured surface, knead lightly until the mixture forms a smooth dough — do not overwork.

Press the shortbread into the prepared tin and mark into 12 wedges. Sprinkle with the extra sugar and bake for 25–30 minutes, or until a light golden colour. Once cool, carefully cut into wedges with a serrated knife and store in an airtight container until required.

To serve, top the mousse cups with a spoonful of whipped cream and dust with cocoa powder. Serve with a wedge of shortbread.

PATISSERIE

In France, a patissier is considered an artist, someone who strives to make their creations as individual as they are. The following recipes are what I would consider a good interpretation of my own individual style — simple, delicious and irresistible.

Blood orange, almond & pistachio cakes

Serves 6

4 blood oranges
250 g (9 oz) unsalted butter, softened
300 g (10^1/$_2$ oz/1^1/$_3$ cups) caster
   (superfine) sugar
6 eggs, separated
1 tablespoon baking powder
75 g (2^1/$_2$ oz) plain (all-purpose) flour
40 g (1^1/$_2$ oz/^{1}/$_4$ cup) shelled,
   unsalted pistachio nuts, blanched
   and skinned
300 g (10^1/$_2$ oz/3 cups) ground
   almonds
45 ml (1^1/$_2$ fl oz) Cointreau
juice of 2 blood oranges
^{1}/$_2$ tablespoon caster (superfine)
   sugar, extra

2 blood oranges, peeled, pith
   and seeds removed, each sliced
   into 6 discs
crème fraîche or sour cream,
   to serve
a small handful of mint leaves,
   to garnish

Put the whole oranges in a large saucepan and cover with water. Invert a plate over the oranges to keep them submerged. Bring to the boil, then reduce the heat and simmer until the oranges are very soft. Drain, then quarter each orange and remove the pulp, discarding the skins and any seeds. Purée briefly in a food processor — you should have about 300 ml (10^1/2 fl oz) of pulp. (Top up with a little water or fresh orange juice if you end up a bit short.)

Preheat the oven to 200°C (400°F/Gas 6). Grease six 10 x 2 cm (4 x ^{3}/4 inch) round cake tins. (You could also use similar-sized shallow tart tins.)

In the bowl of an electric mixer, cream the butter and sugar together until light and pale. Add the egg yolks, one at a time, beating well after each addition. In a separate bowl, sift together the baking powder and flour, then add the pistachios and ground almonds.

Add the orange pulp to the creamed butter mixture, mixing well to combine. Fold in the dry ingredients, then lastly add the Cointreau. Whisk the egg whites in the bowl of an electric mixer until soft peaks form, then carefully fold into the cake mixture. Divide among the prepared tins, place on baking trays and bake for 20–25 minutes, or until a skewer inserted into the centre of the cakes comes out clean.

Meanwhile, combine the blood orange juice and extra sugar in a small saucepan over medium heat and stir until the sugar has dissolved. Bring to the boil, then reduce the heat and simmer until reduced by half, or until the juice begins to thicken. Strain and set aside.

Turn the warm cakes out of the tins onto serving plates. Arrange the blood orange slices on each cake and top with a spoonful of crème fraîche. Drizzle with the strained orange syrup and scatter with the mint leaves.

Apple, rhubarb & ginger pie with Calvados cream

Serves 8

1½ quantities of sweet shortcrust
   pastry (Basics, page 177)

100 g (3½ oz) unsalted butter
6 granny smith apples, peeled, cored
   and thickly sliced
370 g (13 oz/2 cups) soft brown sugar
10 rhubarb stalks, trimmed, strings
   removed, then cut into 3 cm
   (1¼ inch) pieces
1 cinnamon stick
1 vanilla bean, split lengthways,
   seeds scraped
a pinch of freshly grated nutmeg
2 teaspoons grated fresh ginger
grated zest and juice of 1 lemon
40 g (1½ oz/½ cup) fresh white
   breadcrumbs
1 egg, beaten
caster (superfine) sugar,
   for sprinkling

CALVADOS CREAM
250 ml (9 fl oz/1 cup) pouring
   (whipping) cream
2 tablespoons icing (confectioners')
   sugar
60 ml (2 fl oz/¼ cup) Calvados
   (apple liqueur) or brandy

Prepare the pastry as directed and refrigerate for
1 hour before using.

Preheat the oven to 180°C (350°F/Gas 4). Grease a
24 x 4 cm (9½ x 1½ inch) tart tin. Roll out two-thirds
of the chilled pastry 3 mm (⅛ inch) thick and gently
ease into the prepared tin. Refrigerate or freeze for
a further 30 minutes. Roll out the remaining pastry
3 mm (⅛ inch) thick to use as the pie lid, cover with
plastic wrap and refrigerate. Blind-bake the tart base
as directed on page 177 and set aside to cool.

Melt the butter in a heavy-based saucepan over
medium heat. Increase the heat to high, add the apple
slices and cook for 2–3 minutes. Add the brown sugar
and rhubarb and stir to combine. Add the cinnamon
stick, vanilla seeds, nutmeg and ginger and cook until
the apple and rhubarb just begin to soften. Stir in the
lemon zest and juice. Remove from the heat and strain,
reserving the cooking liquid. Spread the apple and
rhubarb mixture in a shallow tray to cool.

If the cooled filling is still quite wet, fold the
breadcrumbs through. Spoon the filling into the blind-
baked pastry case. Brush the edges with beaten egg,
then top with the pastry lid. Trim the edges and crimp
together to seal. Brush the top of the pie with beaten
egg and sprinkle with caster sugar. Make two incisions
in the top of the pie to allow steam to escape, then bake
for 40 minutes, or until golden.

Meanwhile, in a small saucepan, bring the reserved
cooking liquid to the boil, then reduce the heat and
simmer until it reduces to a syrup consistency.
Remove from the heat and set aside.

To make the Calvados cream, whisk the cream and
icing sugar together until soft peaks form. Fold the
Calvados through.

Cut the warm pie into wedges and place in the
centre of serving plates. Drizzle with the reduced syrup
and serve with a spoonful of the Calvados cream.

Mango tartlets with macadamia nut ice cream

Serves 6

500 ml (17 fl oz/2 cups) pouring
(whipping) cream
5 eggs
70 g (2$^1/_2$ oz/scant $^1/_3$ cup) caster
(superfine) sugar
1 vanilla bean, split lengthways,
seeds scraped
3 teaspoons Grand Marnier
six 8 x 2 cm (3$^1/_4$ x $^3/_4$ inch) blind-
baked sweet shortcrust tartlet
cases (Basics, page 177)

RUM CARAMEL
115 g (4 oz/$^1/_2$ cup) caster (superfine)
sugar
2 tablespoons dark rum
2$^1/_2$ tablespoons pouring (whipping)
cream

2 large or 3 small mangoes,
skinned and sliced
icing (confectioners') sugar,
for dusting
macadamia nut ice cream (page 168),
to serve

Preheat the oven to 120°C (235°F/Gas $^1/_2$).

In a large bowl, whisk together the cream, eggs, sugar, vanilla seeds and Grand Marnier. Strain the mixture through a fine sieve into a pouring jug, then carefully pour into the blind-baked tartlet cases. Bake for 40 minutes, or until the filling is set. Remove from the oven and allow to cool to room temperature.

To make the rum caramel, combine the sugar and 125 ml (4 fl oz/$^1/_2$ cup) water in a small saucepan over medium heat and stir until the sugar has dissolved. Bring to the boil and boil, without stirring, until the syrup turns a dark golden colour. Immediately remove from the heat and very carefully, as hot caramel spits, stir in the rum. Add a little more water if the caramel is too thick. Return to the heat, add the cream and stir until the caramel is smooth.

To assemble, arrange the mango slices over the tartlets in a symmetrical pattern and dust liberally with icing sugar. Using a kitchen blowtorch, or under a very hot oven grill (broiler), caramelise the sugar.

Place in the centre of serving plates, drizzle with a little rum caramel and serve with a scoop of macadamia nut ice cream.

Cherry focaccia

Serves 6–8

500 g (1 lb 2 oz) strong flour
   (see Note)
1$^1/_2$ tablespoons dried yeast
1 teaspoon salt
350 ml (12 fl oz) warm water
80 ml (2$^1/_2$ fl oz/$^1/_3$ cup) extra virgin
   olive oil
500 g (1 lb 2 oz) cherries, pitted,
   stems removed
extra virgin olive oil, extra,
   for drizzling
2 tablespoons chopped thyme
   or lemon thyme leaves
50 g (1$^3/_4$ oz/$^1/_4$ cup) caster
   (superfine) sugar
icing (confectioners') sugar,
   for dusting

Put the flour, yeast and salt in the bowl of an electric mixer and, using a dough hook, gradually incorporate the warm water and olive oil. Continue to knead slowly for 15 minutes, or until the dough is smooth and elastic. Alternatively, kneading can be done by hand on a lightly floured surface. Put the dough in a large, lightly oiled bowl, cover the bowl with plastic wrap and leave in a warm place for 15–20 minutes, or until doubled in size.

Place the dough on a floured surface and knock down. Press into a greased 30 x 23 x 4 cm (12 x 9 x 1^1/2 inch) baking tin. Use your fingertips to press in the cherries. Set aside and allow to double in size again.

Preheat the oven to 220°C (425°F/Gas 7). Drizzle the dough liberally with olive oil, scatter with thyme and sprinkle with the sugar. Bake for 15 minutes, or until the dough is cooked and is golden. Serve the cherry focaccia warm or at room temperature, dusted with icing sugar.

NOTE: If strong flour is unavailable you can use plain (all-purpose) flour, but you may need to use about 30 g (1 oz) more as it has less gluten in it. Strong flour is also known as baker's flour.

Banana & passionfruit brioche pizzas

Serves 6

BRIOCHE
1 teaspoon dried yeast
200 g (7 oz) strong flour, sifted
  (see Note)
2 eggs, beaten
2 tablespoons caster (superfine) sugar
60 g (2¹/₄ oz) unsalted butter,
  softened

8 bananas
caster (superfine) sugar, for sprinkling
12 passionfruit, cut in half
thick (double/heavy) cream, to serve
icing (confectioners') sugar,
  for dusting

To make the brioche, put the yeast, flour, eggs, sugar, 2 tablespoons water and a pinch of salt in a large bowl and mix well to combine. Knead, either by hand, or in an electric mixer using a dough hook, for 8–10 minutes, or until the dough is smooth and elastic.

Add the butter and continue to knead until all the butter is incorporated. Cover the bowl with a clean, damp cloth and leave in a warm place for 1 hour, or until doubled in size.

Preheat the oven to 230°C (450°F/Gas 8). Lightly grease six baking trays or six 20–22 cm (8–8¹/2 inch) pizza trays.

Place the dough on a floured surface and knock back. Divide into six even pieces. Roll each piece to a thin 20–22 cm (8–8¹/2 inch) circle and place on the prepared trays. Set aside for a further 20 minutes.

Slice the bananas diagonally and arrange over the pizza bases. Sprinkle with caster sugar and bake two trays at a time for 6–8 minutes, or until the brioche is golden and cooked.

Carefully transfer the hot pizzas to serving plates. Spoon the pulp from the passionfruit over the bananas, dot with small spoonfuls of cream and dust with icing sugar.

NOTE: If strong flour is unavailable you can use plain (all-purpose) flour, but you may need to use about 30 g (1 oz) more as it has less gluten in it. Strong flour is also known as baker's flour.

Mandarin tart

Serves 8

300 ml (10½ fl oz) freshly squeezed
    mandarin juice, strained
150 g (5½ oz/⅔ cup) caster
    (superfine) sugar
200 ml (7 fl oz) pouring (whipping)
    cream
6 eggs
24 x 4 cm (9½ x 1½ inch) blind-
    baked sweet shortcrust pastry case
    (Basics, page 177)

MANDARIN JELLY
300 ml (10½ fl oz) freshly squeezed
    mandarin juice, strained
4 gelatine leaves (8 g/⅙ oz), soaked
    in cold water and squeezed out
50 g (1¾ oz/¼ cup) caster
    (superfine) sugar

Preheat the oven to 110°C (225°F/Gas ½).

Put the mandarin juice in a small saucepan over medium heat. Bring to the boil, then reduce the heat and simmer until reduced by two-thirds. Remove from the heat, add the sugar and stir until the sugar has dissolved. Set aside to cool.

In a bowl, lightly whisk together the cream and eggs. Whisk in the reduced mandarin juice until well combined. Strain the mixture through a fine sieve into a pouring jug, then carefully pour into the blind-baked pastry case. Bake for 55 minutes, or until set. Allow to cool for 10 minutes, then refrigerate until cold.

To make the mandarin jelly, heat 100 ml (3½ fl oz) of the mandarin juice in a small saucepan over low heat. Remove from the heat, whisk in the softened gelatine and stir to completely dissolve. Return to low heat. Add the sugar and remaining mandarin juice and stir until the sugar has dissolved. Remove from the heat and refrigerate until the jelly is just cold — do not allow it to set.

Pour an even layer of jelly over the tart, then carefully return to the refrigerator for several hours, until the jelly has set. Cut into wedges and serve.

Yoghurt citrus cake with fresh cherries

Serves 8

5 eggs, separated
115 g (4 oz/$1/2$ cup) caster (superfine)
   sugar
1 vanilla bean, split lengthways,
   seeds scraped
450 g (1 lb) Greek-style yoghurt
50 g ($13/4$ oz) plain (all-purpose) flour
grated zest and juice of 1 lemon
grated zest of $1/2$ orange

icing (confectioners') sugar,
   for dusting
pitted fresh cherries (stems intact),
   to serve
a half-quantity of cherry syrup
   (Basics, page 180), to serve

Preheat the oven to 170°C (325°F/Gas 3). Grease and line the base and side of a 26 cm (10$1/2$ inch) spring-form cake tin with baking paper.

In a large bowl, whisk the egg yolks, sugar and vanilla seeds until thick and pale. Stir in the yoghurt, then the flour. Add all the citrus zest and juice and mix until well combined.

In the bowl of an electric mixer, whisk the egg whites until stiff peaks form. Fold the beaten egg whites into the yoghurt mixture using a spatula or large spoon.

Pour the cake mixture into the prepared tin. Bake for 40–45 minutes, or until a skewer inserted into the centre of the cake comes out clean. (The cake will rise, then drop back down.) Allow to cool completely in the tin before turning out.

Cut the cake into wedges and dust with icing sugar. Arrange the cherries around and drizzle with cherry syrup.

Caramel tartlets with macadamia nut pastry

Serves 6

MACADAMIA NUT PASTRY
60 g (2$^1/_4$ oz/heaped $^1/_3$ cup) unsalted macadamia nuts, roughly chopped
60 g (2$^1/_4$ oz/$^1/_2$ cup) icing (confectioners') sugar
200 g (7 oz) plain (all-purpose) flour, sifted
200 g (7 oz) unsalted butter, softened

2 x 380 g (13$^1/_2$ oz) tins caramel filling
100 g (3$^1/_2$ oz/$^2/_3$ cup) unsalted macadamia nuts, roasted
icing (confectioners') sugar, for dusting
thick (double/heavy) cream, to serve

To make the macadamia nut pastry, blend the macadamias and icing sugar in a food processor until the nuts resemble course breadcrumbs.

Add the flour and butter and process until the dough begins to come together. Turn out onto a floured surface and bring together using your hands — do not overwork. Wrap in plastic wrap and refrigerate for 1 hour.

Preheat the oven to 180°C (350°F/Gas 4). Grease six 8 x 2 cm (3$^1/4$ x $^3/4$ inch) tartlet tins (this pastry is too soft to roll out into one large tart, so it is best to use individual tartlet tins).

Use your fingers to press the pastry into the prepared tins, 3–4 mm ($^1/8$ inch) thick. Bake for 12–15 minutes, or until cooked and golden in colour. Allow to cool completely in the tins before turning out.

Spoon the caramel into the pastry cases and smooth over the top with the back of a hot metal spoon. Divide the roasted macadamias among the tarts, pressing gently into the caramel. Dust with icing sugar and serve with a spoonful of cream.

These tarts are best served on the day they are made.

Grape & almond tart with muscat

Serves 8

ALMOND PASTRY

**160 g (5¹/₂ oz) unsalted butter,
softened**

**115 g (4 oz/¹/₂ cup) caster (superfine)
sugar**

3 egg yolks

1 teaspoon natural vanilla extract

¹/₂ teaspoon grated lemon zest

**155 g (5¹/₂ oz) plain (all-purpose)
flour, sifted**

¹/₄ teaspoon salt

**100 g (3¹/₂ oz/heaped 1 cup) flaked
almonds, lightly toasted**

CREME PATISSIERE

6 egg yolks

**120 g (4¹/₄ oz/¹/₂ cup) caster
(superfine) sugar**

50 g (1³/₄ oz) plain (all-purpose) flour

1 vanilla bean, split lengthways

500 ml (17 fl oz/2 cups) milk

**300 g (10¹/₂ oz) seedless red grapes,
cut in half**

**45 g (1¹/₂ oz/¹/₂ cup) flaked almonds,
toasted**

60 ml (2 fl oz/¹/₄ cup) muscat liqueur

To make the almond pastry, cream the butter and sugar together in a food processor. Add the egg yolks, vanilla and lemon zest and blend well to combine.

Add the flour, salt and almonds and blend until the pastry just comes together on the blade — do not overwork. Press the pastry 3 mm (1/8 inch) thick into a greased 35 x 12 x 3 cm (14 x 4¹/2 x 1¹/4 inch) tart tin. Refrigerate for 30 minutes before using.

Preheat the oven to 200°C (400°F/Gas 6). Line the pastry with baking paper or foil, fill with pastry weights (such as baking beads, uncooked rice or split peas), then bake for 20 minutes. Reduce the oven temperature to 160°C (315°F/Gas 2–3). Remove the pastry weights and lining and bake for a further 5–8 minutes, or until the pastry is golden. Allow to cool to room temperature.

To make the crème pâtissière, lightly whisk together the egg yolks and sugar, then stir in the flour.

Scrape the seeds from the vanilla bean into a large heavy-based saucepan. Add the vanilla bean and milk and slowly bring to the boil. Remove the vanilla bean. Pour a little of the hot milk into the egg yolk mixture, whisking until smooth. Whisk in the remaining hot milk, then return the mixture to a clean saucepan. Cook over medium heat, stirring continuously, until the mixture has thickened and comes to the boil. Beat for a further minute until smooth, then strain into a clean bowl. Place a sheet of plastic wrap directly on the surface of the crème pâtissière, to prevent a skin forming. Set aside to cool.

To serve, carefully remove the pastry case from the tin and place on a large serving plate. Fill the pastry case with the crème pâtissière. Arrange the grapes over the tart, cut side up, then sprinkle with the toasted flaked almonds and drizzle with the muscat liqueur. Cut into slices and serve. This tart is best served the day it is made.

Blueberry sponge cake with chantilly cream

Serves 8

2 eggs
185 g (6$^1/_2$ oz/heaped $^3/_4$ cup) caster
  (superfine) sugar
50 g (1$^3/_4$ oz) unsalted butter, melted
125 ml (4 fl oz/$^1/_2$ cup) milk
200 g (7 oz) plain (all-purpose) flour
1$^1/_2$ teaspoons baking powder
200 g (7 oz/1$^1/_4$ cups) blueberries

CHANTILLY CREAM
250 ml (9 fl oz/1 cup) pouring
  (whipping) cream
2 tablespoons caster (superfine)
  sugar
$^1/_2$ teaspoon natural vanilla extract

icing (confectioners') sugar,
  for dusting
fresh blueberries, to serve

Preheat the oven to 175°C (345°F/Gas 3–4). Grease and line the base and sides of a 30 x 23 x 4 cm (12 x 9 x 1$^1/2$ inch) baking tin with baking paper.

In a bowl, whisk the eggs and sugar together until thick and pale. Stir in the melted butter and milk until well combined. Sift together the flour and baking powder and fold into the egg mixture.

Pour the sponge mixture into the prepared tin. Scatter the blueberries evenly over the top and bake for 20 minutes, or until a skewer inserted into the centre of the sponge comes out clean. Allow to cool completely in the tin before turning out.

To make the chantilly cream, whisk together the cream, sugar and vanilla until stiff peaks form.

Dust the sponge with icing sugar, cut into squares and serve with the chantilly cream and blueberries. The sponge is best served at room temperature.

Silverbeet, raisin & pine nut tart

Serves 8

90 g (3¹/₄ oz/³/₄ cup) raisins,
  roughly chopped
90 g (3¹/₄ oz/²/₃ cup) currants
80 ml (2¹/₂ fl oz/¹/₃ cup) dark rum
800 g (1 lb 12 oz) silverbeet
  (Swiss chard), stems removed
5 eggs
4 egg yolks
625 ml (21¹/₂ fl oz/2¹/₂ cups) pouring
  (whipping) cream
150 g (5¹/₂ oz/²/₃ cup) caster
  (superfine) sugar
grated zest of 1 orange
2 tablespoons honey
80 g (2³/₄ oz/¹/₂ cup) pine nuts
24 x 4 cm (9¹/₂ x 1¹/₂ inch) blind-
  baked sweet shortcrust pastry case
  (Basics, page 177)
vanilla bean ice cream (page 162),
  to serve

In a small bowl, soak the raisins and currants in the rum overnight.

Preheat the oven to 160°C (315°F/Gas 2–3).

Blanch the silverbeet in boiling salted water for 1 minute, then remove and refresh in iced cold water. Drain and squeeze out any excess moisture. Roughly chop and set aside.

In a large bowl, whisk together the eggs, egg yolks, cream, sugar, orange zest and honey. Stir in the raisins, currants, rum and pine nuts, then fold in the silverbeet.

Pour the silverbeet filling into the blind-baked pastry case. Bake for 40 minutes, or until the filling is set. Remove from the oven and allow to cool to room temperature.

When the tart has cooled, cut into wedges and serve with a scoop of vanilla bean ice cream.

Pear & yoghurt cake with minted yoghurt

Serves 8

220 g (7³/₄ oz) unsalted butter,
   softened
250 g (9 oz/heaped 1 cup) caster
   (superfine) sugar
1 teaspoon natural vanilla extract
3 eggs
375 g (13 oz) self-raising flour,
   sifted
50 ml (1¹/₂ fl oz) milk
250 g (9 oz/1 cup) Greek-style
   yoghurt
3 ripe but firm pears, unpeeled,
   cored and chopped

MINTED YOGHURT
250 g (9 oz/1 cup) Greek-style
   yoghurt
a small handful of mint leaves,
   shredded

Preheat the oven to 170°C (325°F/Gas 3). Grease and line the base and side of a 26 cm (10¹/2 inch) spring-form cake tin with baking paper.

In the bowl of an electric mixer, cream the butter and sugar together until light and pale. Add the vanilla, then the eggs, one at a time, beating well after each addition. Beat in half the sifted flour, then all the milk. Add half the yoghurt and mix well to combine. Gradually add the remaining flour and yoghurt until just combined. Lastly, fold the pears through.

Pour the cake mixture into the prepared tin and bake for 1 hour, or until a skewer inserted into the centre of the cake comes out clean. Allow to cool on a wire rack.

To prepare the minted yoghurt, simply stir half the mint through the yoghurt. Cut the cake into wedges, place on serving plates with a spoonful of the minted yoghurt and garnish with the remaining mint.

Pear & pecan tart with honey & thyme ice cream

Serves 8

1 quantity of sweet shortcrust pastry
(Basics, page 177)
375 ml (13 fl oz/1$^1/_2$ cups) Sauternes
(dessert wine)
3 cardamom pods, roasted, crushed
and sieved
1 cinnamon stick
1 vanilla bean, split lengthways,
seeds scraped
6 ripe but firm pears, cut in half,
cored, then each cut into
8 wedges

FRANGIPANE
250 g (9 oz) unsalted butter, softened
250 g (9 oz/heaped 1 cup) caster
(superfine) sugar
4 eggs
60 g (2$^1/_4$ oz) plain (all-purpose) flour
125 g (4$^1/_2$ oz/1$^1/_4$ cups) ground
almonds
125 g (4$^1/_2$ oz/1 cup) ground pecans

honey and thyme ice cream
(page 163), to serve

Preheat the oven to 180°C (350°F/Gas 4). Prepare the pastry as directed, but only blind-bake for 15 minutes, and do not brush with the beaten egg. Remove from the oven and set aside to cool.

Put the Sauternes, cardamom, cinnamon stick, vanilla bean and vanilla seeds in a large saucepan and bring to the boil. Add the pears and enough water to fully immerse them. Cover with baking paper and a plate to keep the pears completely submerged. Poach gently for 8–10 minutes, or until tender. Allow to cool, leaving the pears in the poaching liquid until required.

Preheat the oven to 150°C (300°F/Gas 2).

To make the frangipane, cream the butter and sugar together in the bowl of an electric mixer until light and pale. Add the eggs, one at a time, beating well after each addition.

In a separate bowl, combine the flour, ground almonds and ground pecans. Fold the dry ingredients into the creamed butter mixture.

Spoon the frangipane into the prepared pastry case and smooth the surface with the back of a hot metal spoon. Using a slotted spoon, remove the pears from the poaching liquid, reserving the liquid. Arrange the pear wedges over the frangipane, fanned out in a symmetrical pattern. Bake for 20 minutes, or until the filling is golden and springs back when touched. Remove from the oven and allow to cool to room temperature.

Meanwhile, strain the pear poaching liquid into a saucepan, discarding the aromatics. Bring back to the boil, then reduce the heat and simmer until reduced to a syrup consistency.

Cut the tart into wedges and place on serving plates. Serve with scoops of honey and thyme ice cream and drizzle with the reduced syrup if desired.

Coffee tea cake with coffee chocolate ice cream

Serves 8

170 g (6 oz) unsalted butter,
   softened
170 g (6 oz/$^3/_4$ cup) caster (superfine)
   sugar
3 eggs
170 g (6 oz) self-raising flour, sifted
3 teaspoons hot espresso or strong
   plunger coffee
coffee chocolate ice cream (page 172),
   to serve

KAHLUA ICING
90 g (3$^1/_4$ oz) unsalted butter,
   softened
90 g (3$^1/_4$ oz/$^1/_3$ cup) cream cheese
250 g (9 oz/2 cups) icing
   (confectioners') sugar
1 teaspoon natural vanilla extract
1 tablespoon Kahlua

Preheat the oven to 170°C (325°F/Gas 3). Grease and line the base and side of a 22 cm (8$^1/2$ inch) round cake tin with baking paper.

In the bowl of an electric mixer, cream the butter and sugar together until light and pale. Add the eggs, one at a time, adding 1 tablespoon of flour after each addition, and beating well. Fold in the remaining flour, then the coffee.

Spoon the cake mixture into the prepared tin and bake for 35–40 minutes, or until a skewer inserted into the centre of the cake comes out clean. Allow the cake to cool in the tin for 30 minutes before turning out onto a wire rack.

Put all the Kahlua icing ingredients in a food processor and blend until smooth. Spread the icing liberally over the cake, then cut the cake into wedges and serve with scoops of coffee chocolate ice cream.

Apple, almond & quince tart

Serves 8

2 sheets of ready-rolled puff pastry
75 g (2¹/₂ oz) unsalted butter
4 large granny smith apples, peeled,
   cored and cut into wedges
2 teaspoons soft brown sugar
75 g (2¹/₂ oz/scant ¹/₃ cup) quince
   paste

FRANGIPANE
125 g (4¹/₂ oz) unsalted butter,
   softened
125 g (4¹/₂ oz/heaped ¹/₂ cup) caster
   (superfine) sugar
2 eggs
30 g (1 oz) plain (all-purpose) flour
125 g (4¹/₂ oz/1¹/₄ cups) ground
   almonds

25 g (1 oz/¹/₄ cup) flaked almonds,
   toasted
vanilla bean ice cream (page 162),
   to serve

Grease and line two baking trays with baking paper. Cut each pastry sheet into a 20 cm (8 inch) round and lay one on each of the prepared trays. Using the tip of a knife, mark a border 2.5 cm (1 inch) in from the outside edge of the pastry, without cutting all the way through. Refrigerate for 30 minutes before using.

Preheat the oven to 200°C (400°F/Gas 6).

To make the frangipane, cream the butter and sugar together in the bowl of an electric mixer until light and pale. Add the eggs, one at a time, beating well after each addition. In a separate bowl, combine the flour and ground almonds. Fold the dry ingredients into the creamed butter mixture.

Using a palette knife or spatula, spread the frangipane in an even layer within the marked border on the pastry bases. Bake for 15–20 minutes, or until the pastry is crisp and golden.

Meanwhile, melt the butter in a large shallow frying pan over medium heat. As the butter begins to foam, add the apple wedges and gently toss until golden on all sides. Add the brown sugar and quince paste and continue to cook until the apples begin to soften. Remove from the heat.

Just before serving, arrange the warm apples over the baked pastry bases and drizzle with the pan juices. Scatter the flaked almonds over the top. Cut the tarts into wedges and serve with scoops of vanilla bean ice cream.

Sweet potato cake with honey & cinnamon cream

Serves 8

190 g (6³/₄ oz) plain (all-purpose)
   flour
1¹/₂ teaspoons baking powder
1 teaspoon salt
1 teaspoon ground nutmeg
1 teaspoon ground cinnamon
185 ml (6 fl oz/³/₄ cup) light olive oil
   or vegetable oil
345 g (12 oz/1¹/₂ cups) caster
   (superfine) sugar
3 eggs
350 g (12 oz/2³/₄ cups) peeled and
   grated orange sweet potato
100 g (3¹/₂ oz/²/₃ cup) pine nuts
ground cinnamon, for dusting
icing (confectioners') sugar,
   for dusting

HONEY & CINNAMON CREAM
250 ml (9 fl oz/1 cup) pouring
   (whipping) cream
1 tablespoon honey
a pinch of ground cinnamon

Preheat the oven to 170°C (325°F/Gas 3). Grease and line the base and side of a 26 cm (10¹/2 inch) spring-form cake tin with baking paper.

Sift the flour, baking powder, salt and spices into a large bowl. In a separate bowl, whisk together the oil and sugar. Add the eggs one at a time, whisking well to combine.

Make a well in the centre of the dry ingredients and add the egg mixture. Mix until well combined, then use a fork to fold in the sweet potato and pine nuts. Pour the cake mixture into the prepared tin and bake for 50 minutes, or until a skewer inserted into the centre of the cake comes out clean. Allow to cool in the tin before turning out onto a wire rack.

To make the honey and cinnamon cream, whisk the cream until soft peaks form, then fold in the honey and cinnamon.

Cut the cake into wedges. Lightly dust with cinnamon and icing sugar and serve with a spoonful of honey and cinnamon cream.

Pine nut & honey tart with orange crème fraîche & raisin syrup

Serves 8

250 g (9 oz) unsalted butter, softened
250 g (9 oz/heaped 1 cup) caster (superfine) sugar
115 g (4 oz/^{1}/$_3$ cup) honey
3 eggs
150 g (5^1/$_2$ oz) plain (all-purpose) flour
a few thyme leaves, chopped
grated zest of 1 orange
250 g (9 oz/1^2/$_3$ cups) pine nuts, toasted
1 blind-baked sweet shortcrust pastry case (Basics, page 177), made using a 35 x 12 x 3 cm (14 x 4^1/$_2$ x 1^1/$_4$ inch) rectangular tart tin

ORANGE CREME FRAICHE
500 g (1 lb 2 oz) crème fraîche or sour cream
^{1}/$_2$ vanilla bean, split lengthways, seeds scraped
grated zest of 1 orange
1^1/$_2$ tablespoons freshly squeezed orange juice
1–2 tablespoons icing (confectioners') sugar

RAISIN SYRUP
200 g (7 oz/1^2/$_3$ cups) raisins
100 g (3^1/$_2$ oz/scant ^{1}/$_2$ cup) caster (superfine) sugar
100 g (3^1/$_2$ oz/scant ^{1}/$_3$ cup) honey
60 ml (2 fl oz/^{1}/$_4$ cup) brandy
grated zest and juice of 2 oranges

Preheat the oven to 170°C (325°F/Gas3).

In the bowl of an electric mixer, cream the butter, sugar, honey and a pinch of salt together until light and pale. Add the eggs, then the flour, mixing well to combine. Transfer the mixture to a bowl. Stir in the thyme, orange zest and pine nuts, then pour into the blind-baked pastry case and bake for 30–35 minutes, or until golden. Remove from the oven and allow to cool to room temperature.

To make the orange crème fraîche, combine the crème fraîche, vanilla seeds, orange zest and orange juice and beat until smooth. Add the icing sugar, to taste. Refrigerate until required.

To make the raisin syrup, place the raisins in a bowl, then combine the remaining ingredients in a small saucepan over medium heat and stir until the sugar has dissolved. Remove from the heat and pour the syrup over the raisins. Set aside to cool.

Cut the tart into wedges and place on serving plates. Spoon the raisins and a little of the syrup over the top. Serve with spoonfuls of orange crème fraîche.

SPECIAL EFFECTS

All our senses contribute to the pleasures of eating, but visual
appeal is a vital one. These desserts are designed to impress.
They'll take some time and patience to prepare, but will ensure
a spectacular finale to a memorable meal.

Liquorice parfait, mango sorbet & sesame wafers

Serves 10

65 g (2¹/₄ oz) good-quality liquorice
250 ml (9 fl oz/1 cup) pouring
   (whipping) cream
4 eggs, separated
60 g (2¹/₄ oz/¹/₄ cup) caster
   (superfine) sugar

NOILLY PRAT CARAMEL
250 g (9 oz/heaped 1 cup) caster
   (superfine) sugar
50 ml (1¹/₂ fl oz) Noilly Prat (dry
   vermouth)

1 quantity of sesame wafers
   (Basics, page 184), made using an
   8 cm (3¹/₄ inch) triangular stencil
mango sorbet (made using the
   fruit sorbet recipe on page 158),
   to serve

Put the liquorice and half the cream in a small saucepan over medium heat and stir until the liquorice dissolves. Remove from the heat. Blend with a hand-held blender until smooth, then allow to cool to room temperature.

Put the egg yolks and half the sugar in a heatproof bowl over a saucepan of simmering water, whisking constantly until doubled in volume. Remove from the heat and continue to whisk until cold.

In the bowl of an electric mixer, whisk the egg whites until soft peaks form, then gradually add the remaining sugar and continue to whisk until all the sugar is used. Lightly whip the remaining cream.

Stir the liquorice mixture into the egg yolk mixture until well combined. Fold in the beaten egg whites, then fold in the whipped cream.

Line a 30 x 12 x 10 cm (12 x 4¹/₂ x 4 inch) triangular terrine mould or rectangular loaf (bar) tin with plastic wrap, allowing a 4 cm (1¹/₂ inch) overhang around the sides. Pour the mixture into the mould, then tap the tin lightly on a work surface to remove air bubbles. Gently cover the top with the overhanging plastic wrap and freeze overnight, or until set.

To make the Noilly Prat caramel, combine the sugar and just enough water to cover in a small heavy-based saucepan over medium heat and stir until the sugar has dissolved. Bring to the boil and boil, without stirring, until the syrup turns a light golden colour. Immediately remove from the heat and very carefully, as hot caramel spits, add the Noilly Prat and 100 ml (3¹/₂ fl oz) water. Return to the heat and stir until smooth. Set aside to cool.

Drizzle the caramel over each serving plate, then lay a sesame wafer in the centre. Turn the parfait out of the mould onto a cutting board. Using a hot knife, cut it into slices about 3 cm (1¹/₄ inches) thick. Place a slice of parfait on the sesame wafer, then sandwich together with another wafer. Serve with a scoop of mango sorbet.

Roasted figs with caramel balsamic ice cream & oatmeal tuiles

Serves 12

OATMEAL TUILES

85 g (3 oz) unsalted butter, softened
60 g (2^1/$_4$ oz/^{1}/$_2$ cup) icing
 (confectioners') sugar
grated zest of 2 lemons
175 g (6 oz/^{1}/$_2$ cup) honey
100 g (3^1/$_2$ oz) plain (all-purpose) flour
50 g (1^3/$_4$ oz/^{1}/$_2$ cup) rolled (porridge)
 oats, lightly toasted

SPICED FIG SYRUP

70 g (2^1/$_2$ oz/scant ^{1}/$_3$ cup) caster
 (superfine) sugar
250 ml (9 fl oz/1 cup) freshly
 squeezed orange juice
175 g (6 oz/1 cup) chopped fresh figs
2 star anise
6 whole black peppercorns

12 large or 18 small fresh figs,
 cut in half
icing (confectioners') sugar,
 for dusting
caramel balsamic ice cream
 (page 165), to serve

Preheat the oven to 160°C (315°F/Gas 2–3).

To make the oatmeal tuiles, cream the butter, sugar and lemon zest together in the bowl of an electric mixer until light and pale. Add the honey and flour and beat until smooth.

Draw three 10 cm (4 inch) circles on a sheet of baking paper and invert the paper over a baking tray. Repeat with another sheet of baking paper and baking tray.

Using a spatula, smear a thin layer of tuile mixture onto each circle, then sprinkle with the rolled oats and bake for 3–5 minutes, or until evenly coloured.

Remove from the oven and, working quickly using a clean palette knife or spatula, carefully remove one tuile and shape it by placing over a rolling pin to curl. Repeat with the second and third tuile — they should all fit on the one rolling pin. If they become too hard to remove, return the tray briefly to the oven to soften.

Repeat the process with the remaining tuile mixture. Allow to cool, then store in an airtight container until required. The tuiles will keep for several days.

To make the spiced fig syrup, combine the sugar and just enough water to cover in a small saucepan over medium heat and stir until the sugar has dissolved. Bring to the boil and boil, without stirring, until the syrup becomes a light golden colour. Immediately remove from the heat and very carefully, as hot caramel spits, add the orange juice. Add the chopped figs, star anise and peppercorns. Return the pan to the heat. Bring to the boil and cook for 3 minutes, then remove from the heat and allow to cool slightly. Strain through a fine sieve, squeezing through as much liquid as possible.

Preheat the oven to 200°C (400°F/Gas 6). Put the figs, cut side up, on a baking tray lined with baking paper. Dust with icing sugar, then roast for 5–8 minutes, or until the figs have begun to caramelise and are golden.

Sit an oatmeal tuile on each serving plate and arrange two or three fig halves in the centre of each tuile. Drizzle with the spiced fig syrup and serve with scoops of caramel balsamic ice cream.

Coffee toffee tiramisu

Serves 8

COFFEE TOFFEE CARAMEL
375 g (13 oz/1^2/$_3$ cups) caster
  (superfine) sugar
1^1/$_2$ tablespoons glucose syrup
2 tablespoons Tia Maria
1^1/$_2$ tablespoons hot espresso
  or strong plunger coffee
125 ml (4 fl oz/^{1}/$_2$ cup) pouring
  (whipping) cream

CREAMED MASCARPONE
500 g (1 lb 2 oz/2^1/$_4$ cups)
  mascarpone cheese
115 g (4 oz/^{1}/$_2$ cup) caster
  (superfine) sugar
6 eggs, separated
250 ml (9 fl oz/1 cup) pouring
  (whipping) cream, lightly whipped

grated good-quality dark
  (bittersweet) chocolate, such as
  couverture, to garnish
savoiardi (lady fingers/sponge finger
  biscuits), or your favourite biscuits
  (cookies), to serve (see Note)

To make the coffee toffee caramel, combine the sugar, glucose syrup and 150 ml (5 fl oz) water in a saucepan over medium heat and stir until the sugar has dissolved. Bring to the boil and boil, without stirring, until the syrup becomes a dark golden colour. Immediately remove from the heat and very carefully, as hot caramel spits, stir in the Tia Maria and coffee. Return to the heat and stir until smooth. Add the cream and bring just to the boil. Remove from the heat and set aside to cool.

To make the creamed mascarpone, put the mascarpone and 1^1/2 tablespoons of the sugar in the bowl of an electric mixer and beat until smooth. In a separate bowl, whisk the egg yolks and another 1^1/2 tablespoons of the sugar together until thick and pale. Fold into the mascarpone mixture.

In a separate bowl, whisk the egg whites until stiff peaks form, then gradually add the remaining sugar and continue to whisk until all the sugar is used. Fold the beaten egg whites into the mascarpone mixture. Lastly, fold in the whipped cream.

To assemble, place a spoonful of the coffee toffee caramel in the base of eight 250–300 ml (9–10^1/2 fl oz) serving glasses. Top with a large spoonful of the creamed mascarpone and continue to layer until the glass is full, finishing with a mascarpone layer. Refrigerate until required. To serve, top with the grated chocolate and serve with savoiardi biscuits for dipping.

NOTE: You can use ready-made savoiardi for this recipe, or see our recipe on page 144.

Caramelised pear terrine, milk gelato & gingerbread

Serves 10

2 kg (4 lb 8 oz) beurre bosc pears,
    peeled, quartered and cored
juice of 2 lemons
500 g (1 lb 2 oz/heaped 2 cups)
    caster (superfine) sugar
125 ml (4 fl oz/$^1/_2$ cup) freshly
    squeezed orange juice
1 cinnamon stick
4 cardamom pods, roasted, crushed
    and sieved
1 vanilla bean, split lengthways,
    seeds scraped
100 ml (3$^1/_2$ fl oz) light-bodied
    dessert wine
grated zest of 1 lime
1 tablespoon freshly squeezed
    lime juice
6 gelatine leaves (12 g/$^1/_4$ oz), soaked
    in cold water and squeezed out

milk gelato (page 159), to serve
1 quantity of gingerbread
    (Basics, page 180), to serve
icing (confectioners') sugar,
    for dusting

Place the pears in a bowl with the lemon juice and enough water to cover (acidulated water will help stop the pears discolouring).

Combine the sugar and 250 ml (9 fl oz/1 cup) water in a large saucepan over medium heat and stir until the sugar has dissolved. Bring to the boil and boil, without stirring, until the syrup becomes a dark golden caramel. Immediately remove from the heat and very carefully, as hot caramel spits, stir in the orange juice. Return to the heat and stir until the caramel is smooth. Remove from the heat, then add the cinnamon stick, cardamom, vanilla bean and vanilla seeds.

Drain the pears. Add them to the caramel, cover with baking paper, then return the saucepan to low heat. Gently simmer, stirring occasionally, until the pears are tender. Remove from the heat and allow to cool slightly.

Using a slotted spoon, remove the pears from the caramel and place in a bowl.

Strain the caramel through a fine sieve, discarding the aromatics. Measure 400 ml (14 fl oz) of caramel and place in a bowl (reserve the remaining caramel to garnish). Add the dessert wine, lime zest and lime juice, then whisk in the softened gelatine and stir to completely dissolve.

Line a 30 x 12 x 10 cm (12 x 4$^1/_2$ x 4 inch) triangular terrine mould or rectangular loaf (bar) tin with plastic wrap, allowing a 4 cm (1$^1/_2$ inch) overhang around the sides.

One by one, lay the pear quarters into the mould to form compact layers, pouring the caramel mixture over each layer. Gently cover the top with the overhanging plastic wrap and freeze overnight, or until set.

Turn the pear terrine out of the mould onto a cutting board and cut into slices about 3 cm (1$^1/_4$ inches) thick. Leave for 5–10 minutes for the terrine to come to room temperature.

Carefully transfer each slice onto serving plates and top with a scoop of milk gelato. Drizzle the reserved caramel around the terrine. Dust the gingerbread with icing sugar and rest against the gelato.

Goat's cheese & honey parfait with candied walnuts & fig chips

Serves 8–10

140 g (5 oz/²/₃ cup) caster
  (superfine) sugar
2 tablespoons honey
6 egg yolks
450 ml (16 fl oz) pouring (whipping)
  cream, lightly whipped
4 tablespoons fresh soft goat's
  cheese

FIG CHIPS
2 large or 3 medium fresh figs
icing (confectioners') sugar,
  for dusting

1 quantity of walnut praline
  (Basics, page 184)
1 quantity of candied walnuts
  (Basics, page 177)
1 quantity of balsamic syrup
  (Basics, page 176)

Combine the sugar, honey and 80 ml (2¹/₂ fl oz/¹/₃ cup) water in a small saucepan over medium heat and stir until the sugar has dissolved. Bring to the boil, then reduce the heat and simmer, stirring constantly, for 16–20 minutes, or until the temperature reaches 120°C (248°F) on a sugar thermometer, or the mixture reaches the soft-ball stage.

Meanwhile, lightly whisk the egg yolks in the bowl of an electric mixer. When the sugar syrup reaches 120°C (248°F), gradually add it to the egg yolks in a constant steady stream, whisking constantly until cold. Use a whisk to carefully fold in the cream, then the goat's cheese.

Line a 28 x 10 x 8 cm (11¹/₄ x 4 x 3¹/₄ inch) rectangular loaf (bar) tin with plastic wrap, allowing a 4 cm (1¹/₂ inch) overhang around the sides. Spoon the parfait mixture into the mould, then tap the tin lightly on a work surface to remove air bubbles. Gently cover with the overhanging plastic wrap and freeze overnight, or until set.

Preheat the oven to 60–70°C (140–150°F/Gas ¹/₄), or as low as your oven will go. Grease and line a baking tray with baking paper and sprinkle liberally with icing sugar.

To make the fig chips, use a mandolin or sharp knife to finely slice the figs. Arrange in a single layer on the prepared tray, dust with icing sugar and bake for several hours, until the fig slices have dried out and are crisp. Cool and store in an airtight container until required.

Put the walnut praline pieces in a food processor and crush to a fine texture, using the pulse button.

Lay some plastic wrap on a flat work surface and cover with an even layer of the crushed praline. Turn the parfait out of the mould and place lengthways at one end of the plastic wrap, over the praline. Roll the parfait over the praline, wrapping with the plastic as you go. Continue to roll and wrap the parfait until all sides are covered with praline and plastic wrap. Freeze for at least 30 minutes before serving.

Carefully remove the plastic wrap from the parfait then, using a hot knife, cut it into slices about 3 cm (1¹/₄ inches) thick. Place a slice in the centre of each plate, then scatter with the fig chips and candied walnuts. Use a hot teaspoon to drizzle a little balsamic syrup around each serving plate.

Vanilla-scented peaches, toasted brioche & mascarpone

Serves 6

170 g (6 oz/$^3/_4$ cup) caster (superfine)
    sugar
6 large or 9 medium ripe but firm
    peaches, quartered and stones
    removed
1 vanilla bean, split lengthways,
    seeds scraped, or 1 teaspoon
    natural vanilla extract
2 tablespoons brandy
juice of 1 lemon
a knob of unsalted butter
6 slices of brioche, each about
    1.5 cm ($^5/_8$ inch) thick

mascarpone cheese, to serve
icing (confectioners') sugar,
    for dusting

Combine the sugar and 80 ml (2$^1/_2$ fl oz/$^1/_3$ cup) water in a heavy-based saucepan over medium heat and stir until the sugar has dissolved. Bring to the boil and boil, without stirring, until the syrup becomes a light golden colour. Immediately remove from the heat, then add the peaches and vanilla seeds or extract.

Return to medium heat and continue to cook until the peaches just begin to soften, adding more water if necessary to maintain a syrup consistency. Remove from the heat and gently stir in the brandy, lemon juice and butter.

Preheat the oven grill (broiler) to high. Toast the brioche lightly on both sides, cut the slices diagonally in half and arrange in the centre of serving plates. Spoon the peaches and syrup over the brioche and top with a small spoonful of mascarpone. Dust with icing sugar.

Iced coconut parfait, pineapple sorbet & pineapple & lime salsa

Serves 10

115 g (4 oz/$1/2$ cup) caster (superfine)
   sugar
500 ml (17 fl oz/2 cups) coconut milk
50 g ($13/4$ oz) glucose syrup
juice of 3 limes
3 gelatine leaves (6 g/$1/8$ oz), soaked
   in cold water and squeezed out
grated zest of 1 lime

COCONUT SYRUP
440 ml ($151/2$ fl oz) tin coconut cream
2 tablespoons caster (superfine)
   sugar

PINEAPPLE & LIME SALSA
$1/2$ pineapple, core removed,
   finely diced
juice of 1 lime
grated zest of $1/2$ lime
1 makrut (kaffir lime) leaf, finely
   sliced
1 teaspoon diced red chilli
a few mint leaves, finely sliced

10 sesame wafers (Basics, page 184)
pineapple sorbet (page 158),
   to serve
shaved fresh coconut, to garnish

Put the sugar and 100 ml ($31/2$ fl oz) of the coconut milk in a heavy-based saucepan over medium heat and stir until the sugar has dissolved. Add the glucose syrup, lime juice and remaining coconut milk and bring to the boil. Remove from the heat. Whisk in the softened gelatine and stir to completely dissolve. Refrigerate until cold, then churn in an ice cream machine according to the manufacturer's instructions. Once fully churned, add the lime zest. Alternatively, transfer to a shallow metal tray and freeze, whisking every couple of hours until creamy and frozen.

Line a 30 x 12 x 10 cm (12 x $41/2$ x 4 inch) triangular terrine mould or rectangular loaf (bar) tin with plastic wrap, allowing a 4 cm ($11/2$ inch) overhang around the sides. Spoon the churned iced coconut parfait into the mould, then tap lightly on a work surface to remove air bubbles. Gently cover the top with the overhanging plastic wrap and freeze overnight, or until set.

To make the coconut syrup, combine the coconut cream and sugar in a saucepan over medium heat and stir until the sugar has dissolved. Bring to the boil, then reduce the heat and simmer until the mixture reduces to a syrup consistency. Remove from the heat, allow to cool, then refrigerate until required.

Combine all the pineapple and lime salsa ingredients in a bowl and set aside for 15 minutes for the flavours to infuse.

To serve, place a spoonful of the salsa on each plate. Turn the coconut parfait out of the mould onto a cutting board. Using a hot knife, cut into slices about 3 cm ($11/4$ inch) thick and place a slice over the salsa. Sit a sesame wafer over the parfait and place a scoop of pineapple sorbet on top. Drizzle the coconut syrup around the plate and garnish with shaved coconut.

Spiced quince trifle

Serves 6

1 quantity of poached quince
   (Basics, page 181)
750 ml (26 fl oz/3 cups) red wine
8 gelatine leaves (16 g/$^1/_2$ oz), soaked
   in cold water and squeezed out
100 g (3$^1/_2$ oz) savoiardi (lady fingers/
   sponge finger biscuits) (see Note)

300 ml (10$^1/_2$ fl oz) pouring (whipping)
   cream, whipped
70 g (2$^1/_2$ oz/$^1/_2$ cup) hazelnuts,
   roasted, skinned and finely
   chopped
a few basil leaves, finely sliced
a few mint leaves, finely sliced

Prepare the poached quince as directed. Measure out 700 ml (24 fl oz) of the poaching syrup and set aside.

Heat the wine in a saucepan over medium heat, bring to the boil, then reduce the heat and simmer until reduced by half. Remove from the heat.

In a clean saucepan, combine the reserved quince syrup and the reduced wine and bring to the boil. Whisk in the softened gelatine and stir to completely dissolve. Remove from the heat, strain, then set aside to cool.

Arrange the savoiardi in the base of individual serving glasses or bowls, breaking them to fit. Pour in enough of the red wine jelly mixture to cover. Allow the biscuits to absorb the jelly for 2–3 minutes, then add half the quince wedges. Refrigerate for several hours, or until set. Dice and reserve the remaining quince to garnish.

To serve, spoon the diced quince over the jelly, top with a spoonful of cream and scatter with the hazelnuts, basil and mint.

NOTE: You can use ready-made savoiardi for this recipe, or see our recipe on page 144.

Zabaione with savoiardi

Serves 6

SAVOIARDI

2 eggs
125 ml (4 fl oz/$^1/_2$ cup) olive oil
170 g (6 oz/$^3/_4$ cup) caster (superfine) sugar
1 teaspoon natural vanilla extract
grated zest of 1 orange
1 tablespoon freshly squeezed orange juice
450–500 g (1 lb–1lb 2 oz) self-raising flour
icing (confectioners') sugar, for dusting

ZABAIONE

8 egg yolks
75 g (2$^1/_2$ oz/$^1/_3$ cup) caster (superfine) sugar
200 ml (7 fl oz) Marsala or good-quality sweet sherry

Preheat the oven to 180°C (350°F/Gas 4). Grease and line several baking trays with baking paper.

To make the savoiardi, whisk together the eggs, olive oil, sugar, vanilla, orange zest and orange juice in a large bowl. Gradually add enough flour so the mixture comes together to form a soft dough. Cut the dough into three pieces. Roll each piece on a floured surface into a cylinder shape, about 2 cm ($^3/4$ inch) thick. Cut the dough on an angle into 6 cm (2$^1/2$ inch) lengths.

Lightly toss the savoiardi in icing sugar and place on the prepared trays 3–4 cm (1$^1/4$–1$^1/2$ inches) apart to allow for spreading. Bake for 10–12 minutes, or until golden. Allow to cool completely on the trays. Savoiardi will keep for several days stored in an airtight container.

Put the zabaione ingredients in a heatproof bowl over a saucepan of simmering water, whisking constantly until the mixture becomes thick and foamy and doubles in volume. Divide among six large martini-style serving glasses and serve immediately, with one or two savoiardi each.

Caramel soufflés

Serves 6

melted unsalted butter, for brushing
caster (superfine) sugar
6 egg whites
1 x 380 g (13$^1/_2$ oz) tin caramel filling

icing (confectioners') sugar, for
   dusting
vanilla bean ice cream (page 162),
   to serve

Preheat the oven to 180°C (350°F/Gas 4). Brush six 185 ml (6 fl oz/$^3/4$ cup) ceramic soufflé dishes with melted butter, then dust with caster sugar, shaking out any excess.

Measure the egg whites in a measuring jug, then transfer to the bowl of an electric mixer. Measure exactly the same amount of caster sugar by volume — so if you have $^1/2$ cup egg whites, you will need $^1/2$ cup sugar. Whisk the egg whites until soft peaks form, then gradually add the sugar and continue to whisk until all the sugar is used.

Spoon about 1 teaspoon of the caramel filling into the bottom of each soufflé dish. Put the remainder in a mixing bowl and, using a large balloon whisk, briskly whisk in a large spoonful of the beaten egg whites. Gently fold in the remaining egg whites — do not overwork.

Spoon the mixture into the soufflé dishes, levelling off the top with a spatula. Gently run your thumb or a paring knife around the inside rim of each dish to loosen the mixture away from the top — this will allow the soufflés to rise cleanly.

Bake for 10–12 minutes, or until the soufflés have risen about 1–2 cm ($^1/2$–$^3/4$ inch) out of the dishes and are well coloured.

Dust the soufflés with icing sugar and place on serving plates. Serve immediately with a scoop of vanilla bean ice cream.

Passionfruit soufflé with passionfruit ice cream

Serves 6

melted unsalted butter,
  for brushing
75 g (2¹/₂ oz/¹/₃ cup) caster
  (superfine) sugar, plus extra,
  for dusting
250 ml (9 fl oz/1 cup) passionfruit
  pulp, strained, reserving
  1 teaspoon of seeds (see Note)
35 g (1¹/₄ oz/heaped ¹/₄ cup)
  cornflour (cornstarch)
6 egg whites

icing (confectioners') sugar,
  for dusting
passionfruit ice cream (page 163),
  to serve

Brush six 185 ml (6 fl oz/³/4 cup) ceramic soufflé dishes with melted butter, then dust with caster sugar, shaking out any excess.

Combine the caster sugar and 50 ml (1¹/2 fl oz) water in a small saucepan over medium heat and stir until the sugar has dissolved. Add the strained passionfruit pulp. Bring to the boil, then reduce the heat and simmer until reduced by half.

Mix the cornflour with 3 teaspoons of water to make a smooth paste, then drizzle into the passionfruit reduction, stirring constantly until smooth. Remove from the heat. Add the reserved passionfruit seeds. Transfer to a large mixing bowl and set aside to cool to room temperature.

Preheat the oven to 180°C (350°F/Gas 4).

Measure the egg whites in a measuring jug, then transfer to the bowl of an electric mixer. Measure exactly the same amount of caster sugar by volume — so if you have ¹/2 cup egg whites, you will need ¹/2 cup sugar. Whisk the egg whites until soft peaks form, then gradually add the sugar and continue to whisk until all the sugar is used.

Using a large balloon whisk, briskly whisk a large spoonful of the egg whites into the passionfruit reduction. Gently fold in the remaining egg whites — do not overwork.

Spoon the mixture into the soufflé dishes, levelling off the top with a spatula. Gently run your thumb or a paring knife around the inside rim of each dish to loosen the mixture away from the top — this will allow the soufflés to rise cleanly.

Bake for 10–12 minutes, or until the soufflés have risen about 1–2 cm (¹/2–³/4 inch) out of the dishes and are well coloured.

Dust the soufflés with icing sugar and place on serving plates. Serve immediately with a scoop of passionfruit ice cream.

NOTE: Fresh passionfruit pulp is preferable for this recipe, although it is sometimes also available frozen.

Hazelnut meringue & raspberry mousse

Serves 6

RASPBERRY MOUSSE
185 g (6^1/$_2$ oz/1^1/$_4$ cups) chopped
   good-quality white chocolate,
   such as couverture
2 egg whites
50 g (1^3/$_4$ oz/^{1}/$_4$ cup) caster
   (superfine) sugar
375 ml (13 fl oz/1^1/$_2$ cups) pouring
   (whipping) cream, lightly whipped
1 quantity of raspberry coulis
   (Basics, page 183)

HAZELNUT MERINGUE
4 egg whites
190 g (6^3/$_4$ oz/heaped ^{3}/$_4$ cup) caster
   (superfine) sugar
95 g (3^1/$_2$ oz/heaped ^{3}/$_4$ cup) ground
   hazelnuts
2 tablespoons plain (all-purpose) flour

unsweetened cocoa powder,
   for dusting
fresh raspberries, to serve

To make the raspberry mousse, put the chocolate in a heatproof bowl over a saucepan of simmering water and allow to melt, stirring occasionally, until smooth. Allow to cool to room temperature.

In the bowl of an electric mixer, whisk the egg whites until soft peaks form, then gradually add the sugar and continue to whisk until all the sugar has been used.

Fold the cooled chocolate into the beaten egg whites, then fold in the whipped cream and 3 tablespoons of the raspberry coulis. Reserve the remaining raspberry coulis to garnish.

Transfer the mixture to a glass or ceramic dish, cover with plastic wrap and refrigerate for several hours.

Preheat the oven to 180°C (350°F/Gas 4). Draw six 8 cm (3^1/4 inch) circles, well spaced, on two sheets of baking paper. Grease two baking trays and invert the sheets of baking paper over them.

To make the hazelnut meringue, whisk the egg whites in the bowl of an electric mixer until soft peaks form. Gradually add 65 g (2^1/4 oz/heaped ^{1}/4 cup) of the sugar and continue to whisk until all the sugar has been used.

In a separate bowl, combine the remaining sugar with the ground hazelnuts and flour, mixing well. Fold into the beaten egg whites.

Use a small palette knife to spread the meringue evenly onto the circles on the prepared trays.

Bake for 12–15 minutes, or until the meringues are golden and firm. Remove from the oven and set aside to cool completely. Repeat with the remaining meringue mixture to make 12 discs. Store the meringues in an airtight container until required.

To serve, place a small spoonful of raspberry mousse in the centre of each serving plate and top with a meringue. Spread 2 spoonfuls of mousse over the meringue, then top with another meringue. Finish with a spoonful of mousse on top and dust with cocoa powder. Drizzle the reserved raspberry coulis around the plate and scatter with raspberries.

Frozen zuccotto

Serves 6

1 quantity of vanilla bean ice cream
(page 162)
240 g (8$^1/_2$ oz/1$^2/_3$ cups) chopped
good-quality dark (bittersweet)
chocolate, such as couverture
2 eggs
2 egg yolks
115 g (4 oz/$^1/_2$ cup) caster (superfine)
sugar
1 tablespoon Cointreau
360 ml (12$^1/_2$ fl oz) pouring (whipping)
cream, lightly whipped
100 g (3$^1/_2$ oz) amaretti (almond
cookies) or savoiardi (lady fingers/
sponge finger biscuits), roughly
chopped (see Note)
140 g (5 oz/1 cup) hazelnuts, roasted,
skinned and roughly chopped
155 g (5$^1/_2$ oz/1 cup) whole blanched
almonds, roasted and roughly
chopped
95 g (3$^1/_4$ oz/$^1/_2$ cup) mixed peel

ORANGE SYRUP
115 g (4 oz/$^1/_2$ cup) caster (superfine)
sugar
grated zest of 1 orange

Remove the ice cream from the freezer for 5 minutes
to soften slightly.

Sit an 18 x 10 cm (7 x 4 inch) bowl (or one of a similar
size) in a larger bowl filled with ice. Use the back of a
metal spoon to line the bowl with a 2 cm ($^3/_4$ inch)
thick layer of ice cream, working quickly so it doesn't
melt. Freeze for several hours, until set. Check the ice
cream regularly to make sure it doesn't lose its shape
— smooth over with the back of the spoon if necessary.

Put the chocolate in a heatproof bowl over a
saucepan of simmering water and allow to melt,
stirring occasionally, until smooth. Remove from
the heat and set aside to cool.

In a bowl, whisk the eggs, egg yolks and sugar
together until thick and pale. Stir in the cooled
chocolate and Cointreau and mix well to combine.
Using a large whisk, gently fold in the cream. Lastly,
fold in the biscuits, hazelnuts, almonds and mixed peel.

Remove the ice cream bowl from the freezer. Spoon
the chocolate mixture into the centre of the bowl and
smooth over the top using the back of a hot metal
spoon. Cover with baking paper and freeze overnight,
or until set.

To make the orange syrup, combine the sugar and
125 ml (4 fl oz/$^1/_2$ cup) water in a small saucepan over
medium heat and stir until the sugar has dissolved.
Bring to the boil, add the orange zest, then reduce the
heat and simmer for 5 minutes. Remove from the heat
and set aside to cool. Refrigerate until required.

Remove the zuccotto from the freezer 1–2 hours
before serving. Remove the baking paper and briefly
submerge the bowl in another bowl of hot water, as
close to the top as possible, to loosen slightly. Invert
a flat plate or chopping board over the top of the bowl
and turn the zuccotto out. Return to the freezer
until required.

To serve, slice the zuccotto into wedges using a hot
knife and arrange on serving plates. Spoon the orange
syrup around and serve immediately.

NOTE: You can use ready-made savoiardi for this
recipe, or see our recipe on page 144.

Nougat glacé with hazelnuts & almonds

Serves 10

75 g (2^1/$_2$ oz/scant ^{1}/$_2$ cup) mixed
  dried fruit
70 g (2^1/$_2$ oz/^{1}/$_3$ cup) glacé cherries,
  chopped
2^1/$_2$ tablespoons Grand Marnier
115 g (4 oz/^{1}/$_2$ cup) caster (superfine)
  sugar
35 g (1^1/$_4$ oz/^{1}/$_4$ cup) hazelnuts,
  roasted and skinned
35 g (1^1/$_4$ oz/^{1}/$_4$ cup) whole blanched
  almonds, roasted
grated zest of 1 lime
2 tablespoons caster (superfine)
  sugar, extra
2 tablespoons honey
35 g (1 oz) glucose syrup
3 egg whites
375 ml (13 fl oz/1^1/$_2$ cups) pouring
  (whipping) cream, lightly whipped

FRUIT SYRUP
115 g (4 oz/^{1}/$_2$ cup) caster (superfine)
  sugar
95 g (3^1/$_4$ oz/^{1}/$_2$ cup) mixed dried
  fruit, roughly chopped
2^1/$_2$ tablespoons Grand Marnier

Soak the mixed dried fruit and glacé cherries in the Grand Marnier for several hours, or overnight.

Grease and line a baking tray with baking paper.

Combine the sugar and just enough water to cover in a heavy-based saucepan over medium heat and stir until the sugar has dissolved. Bring to the boil and boil, without stirring, until the syrup becomes a dark golden colour. Immediately remove from the heat and add the nuts and lime zest. Quickly pour the mixture over the prepared tray and flatten out using the back of a hot metal spoon. Allow to cool. Once cold, break the praline into pieces in a mortar and pestle, or break up in a food processor, using the pulse button.

Combine the extra sugar, honey and glucose syrup in a heavy-based saucepan over medium heat and stir until the sugar has dissolved. Bring to the boil, then reduce the heat and simmer, stirring constantly, for 15–20 minutes, or until the temperature reaches 120°C (248°F) on a sugar thermometer, or the mixture reaches the soft-ball stage.

Meanwhile, whisk the egg whites in the bowl of an electric mixer until stiff peaks form. When the sugar syrup reaches 120°C (248°F), gradually add it to the beaten egg whites in a constant steady stream, whisking constantly until cold. Use a whisk to carefully fold the cream, macerated fruit and praline into the meringue.

Line a 30 x 12 x 10 cm (12 x 4^1/2 x 4 inch) triangular terrine mould or rectangular loaf (bar) tin with plastic wrap, allowing a 4 cm (1^1/2 inch) overhang around the sides. Spoon the nougat mixture into the mould, then tap the tin lightly on a work surface to remove air bubbles. Gently cover the top with the overhanging plastic wrap and freeze overnight, or until set.

To make the fruit syrup, combine the sugar and 125 ml (4 fl oz/^{1}/2 cup) water in a small saucepan and stir until the sugar has dissolved. Bring to the boil, then remove from the heat. Stir in the dried fruit and Grand Marnier and set aside to cool.

Turn the nougat glacé out of the mould onto a cutting board. Using a hot knife, cut it into slices about 1.5 cm (^{5}/8 inch) thick and arrange two slices in the centre of each serving plate. Spoon the fruit syrup over and around the plate, or serve separately.

ICED DELIGHTS

A simple bowl of rich, creamy home-made ice cream is sometimes all you need to satisfy those sweet cravings. Serve these ice creams, sorbets, gelatos and granitas on their own, with your favourite biscuit (cookie), or to accompany many of the wonderful desserts featured in this book.

Green apple sorbet with apple crisps

Serves 6

500 g (1 lb 2 oz) granny smith apples, unpeeled, cored and quartered
juice of 1/2 lemon
250 g (9 oz/heaped 1 cup) caster (superfine) sugar
3 teaspoons Calvados (apple liqueur) or brandy, optional
juice of 3 lemons, extra

APPLE CRISPS
2 granny smith apples, peeled and cored
lemon juice
caster (superfine) sugar, for dusting

Toss the apple quarters in the lemon juice to stop them browning, then place in a sealed container with the juice and freeze overnight.

Combine the sugar and 250 ml (9 fl oz/1 cup) water in a heavy-based saucepan over medium heat and stir until the sugar has dissolved. Bring to the boil, then remove the sugar syrup from the heat and cool. Refrigerate until cold.

Put the frozen apples, sugar syrup, Calvados (if using) and extra lemon juice in a food processor and blend to a smooth purée. Taste the mixture — if it is too sweet, add more lemon juice to taste. Churn the mixture in an ice cream machine according to the manufacturer's instructions, then store in the freezer until needed. Alternatively, transfer to a shallow metal tray and freeze, whisking every couple of hours until smooth and frozen.

Preheat the oven to 60–70°C (140–150°F/Gas 1/4), or as low as your oven will go. Grease and line a baking tray with baking paper.

To make the apple crisps, use a mandolin or slicer to shave the apples into very thin slices. Brush the apple slices on both sides with lemon juice, then lay them in a single layer on the prepared tray. Dust with caster sugar and dry in the oven for several hours, until the apple slices are crisp. Cool and store in an airtight container until required. (They will stay crisp for 1–2 days.)

Scoop the apple sorbet into serving bowls and serve with the apple crisps.

Fruit sorbet

Makes about 1 litre (35 fl oz)

460 g (1 lb/2 cups) caster (superfine)
   sugar
500 ml (17 fl oz/2 cups) fruit purée,
   such as mango, strawberry or
   raspberry (see Note)

Combine the sugar and 500 ml (17 fl oz/2 cups) water in a saucepan over medium heat and stir until the sugar has dissolved. Bring to the boil, then remove from the heat and add the fruit purée. Refrigerate until cold.

Transfer to an ice cream machine, churn according to the manufacturer's instructions, then freeze. Alternatively, transfer to a shallow metal tray and freeze, whisking every couple of hours until smooth and frozen.

NOTE: Fruit purées are available from good delicatessens and food emporiums. If using fresh or frozen strawberries or raspberries, purée the fruit in a food processor until smooth, then strain through a fine sieve, forcing the mixture through the sieve with the back of a spoon to remove the seeds.

Pineapple sorbet

Makes 1.5 litres (52 fl oz)

500 g (1 lb 2 oz/heaped 2 cups)
   caster (superfine) sugar
800 ml (28 fl oz) strained fresh
   pineapple juice (see Note)

Combine the sugar and 500 ml (17 fl oz/2 cups) water in a saucepan over medium heat and stir until the sugar has dissolved. Bring to the boil, then remove from the heat and add the pineapple juice. Refrigerate until cold.

Transfer to an ice cream machine, churn according to the manufacturer's instructions, then freeze. Alternatively, transfer to a shallow metal tray and freeze, whisking every couple of hours until smooth and frozen.

NOTE: To prepare the pineapple juice, dice the flesh from two fresh pineapples. Juice the pineapple flesh using a vegetable juicer, or purée in a food processor, then pass through a sieve before measuring the required quantity. You can also used bottled pineapple juice, preferably with no added sugar.

Milk gelato

Makes about 1 litre (35 fl oz)

175 g (6 oz/$^3/_4$ cup) caster (superfine) sugar
100 g (3$^1/_2$ oz) glucose syrup
700 ml (24 fl oz) milk

Combine the sugar, glucose syrup and 250 ml (9 fl oz/ 1 cup) of the milk in a large saucepan over medium heat and stir until the sugar has dissolved — do not allow to boil. Remove from the heat. Stir in the remaining milk, then refrigerate until cold.

Transfer to an ice cream machine, churn according to the manufacturer's instructions, then freeze. Alternatively, transfer to a shallow metal tray and freeze, whisking every couple of hours until creamy and frozen.

Yoghurt gelato

Makes 1.25 litres (44 fl oz)

350 ml (12 fl oz) milk
175 g (6 oz/$^3/_4$ cup) caster (superfine) sugar
75 g (2$^1/_2$ oz/$^1/_3$ cup) glucose syrup
500 ml (17 fl oz/2 cups) Greek-style yoghurt
juice of $^1/_2$ lemon

Combine the milk, sugar and glucose syrup in a heavy-based saucepan over medium heat and stir until the sugar has dissolved. Bring to the boil, then remove from the heat and set aside to cool completely.

Put the yoghurt in a large mixing bowl. Whisk the cooled milk mixture into the yoghurt, then whisk in the lemon juice. Refrigerate until cold.

Transfer to an ice cream machine, churn according to the manufacturer's instructions, then freeze. Alternatively, transfer to a shallow metal tray and freeze, whisking every couple of hours until creamy and frozen.

Lychee & mint granita with glass biscuits

Serves 6

100 g (3^1/$_2$ oz/scant ^{1}/$_2$ cup) caster
   (superfine) sugar
1.5 kg (3 lb 5 oz) fresh lychees, peeled
   and seeded, or 750 g (1 lb 10 oz)
   drained tinned lychees
a small handful of mint leaves,
   roughly chopped

GLASS BISCUITS
50 g (1^3/$_4$ oz) unsalted butter
90 g (3^1/$_4$ oz/heaped ^{1}/$_3$ cup) caster
   (superfine) sugar
45 g (1^1/$_2$ oz) glucose syrup
45 g (1^1/$_2$ oz) plain (all-purpose) flour

Combine the sugar and 250 ml (9 fl oz/1 cup) water in a large saucepan over medium heat and stir until the sugar has dissolved. Bring to the boil, then remove from the heat. Add the lychees and allow to cool to room temperature.

Purée the lychees and sugar syrup in a food processor or upright blender until smooth. Pour the mixture into a shallow metal tray and freeze for several hours until set.

To make the glass biscuits, put the butter, sugar and glucose syrup in a small saucepan over low heat, stirring constantly until just melted. Transfer to a mixing bowl and add the flour. Stir until the mixture comes together, then set aside to cool. Refrigerate the biscuit mixture for 1 hour before using.

Preheat the oven to 160°C (315°F/Gas 2–3). Grease and line several baking trays with baking paper.

With lightly wetted hands, shape the biscuit mixture into marble-sized balls, about 2 cm (^{3}/4 inch) in diameter. Place on the prepared trays, leaving 5 cm (2 inches) in between to allow for spreading. Bake for 10 minutes, or until lightly golden. Remove from the oven and allow to cool on the trays, before storing in a sealed container. Glass biscuits will keep for several days.

To serve, remove the lychee mixture from the freezer and scratch the surface with a fork to form a granita. Stir the mint through.

Spoon the granita into serving glasses. Serve immediately with glass biscuits.

Vanilla bean ice cream

Makes 1.25 litres (44 fl oz)

12 egg yolks
300 g (10^1/$_2$ oz/1^1/$_3$ cups) caster
(superfine) sugar
2 vanilla beans, split lengthways
500 ml (17 fl oz/2 cups) milk
500 ml (17 fl oz/2 cups) pouring
(whipping) cream

In a bowl, lightly whisk together the egg yolks and sugar. Scrape the seeds from the vanilla beans into a large saucepan. Add the vanilla beans, milk and cream and bring almost to the boil. Whisk the hot milk mixture into the egg yolks, then return to a clean saucepan over medium heat.

Using a wooden spoon, stir constantly until the custard thickens and coats the back of the spoon. Do not let it boil. Strain through a fine sieve, allow to cool to room temperature, then refrigerate until cold.

Transfer to an ice cream machine, churn according to the manufacturer's instructions, then freeze. Alternatively, transfer to a shallow metal tray and freeze, whisking every couple of hours until creamy and frozen.

Crème fraîche ice cream

Makes 1.25 litres (44 fl oz)

5 egg yolks
1 litre (35 fl oz/4 cups) milk
300 g (10^1/$_2$ oz/1^1/$_3$ cups) caster
(superfine) sugar
70 g (2^1/$_2$ oz/scant ^{1}/$_3$ cup) glucose
syrup
335 g (11^3/$_4$ oz) crème fraîche
200 ml (7 fl oz) pouring (whipping)
cream

In a bowl, lightly whisk the egg yolks. Combine the milk, sugar and glucose syrup in a large saucepan over medium heat and stir until the sugar has dissolved. Bring almost to the boil, then remove from the heat. Whisk the hot milk mixture into the egg yolks, then return to a clean saucepan over medium heat.

Using a wooden spoon, stir constantly until the custard thickens and coats the back of the spoon. Do not let it boil. Strain through a fine sieve, allow to cool to room temperature, then refrigerate until cold.

Whisk the crème fraîche and cream into the custard. Transfer to an ice cream machine, churn according to the manufacturer's instructions, then freeze. Alternatively, transfer to a shallow metal tray and freeze, whisking every couple of hours until creamy and frozen.

Passionfruit ice cream

Makes about 1 litre (35 fl oz)

6 egg yolks
150 g (5$1/2$ oz/$2/3$ cup) caster (superfine) sugar
500 ml (17 fl oz/2 cups) pouring (whipping) cream
200 ml (7 fl oz) passionfruit pulp, strained (see Note)

In a bowl, lightly whisk together the egg yolks and sugar. Heat the cream in a large saucepan and bring almost to the boil. Whisk the hot cream into the egg yolks, add the passionfruit pulp, then return to a clean saucepan over medium heat.

Using a wooden spoon, stir constantly until the custard thickens and coats the back of the spoon. Do not let it boil. Strain through a fine sieve, allow to cool to room temperature, then refrigerate until cold.

Transfer to an ice cream machine, churn according to the manufacturer's instructions, then freeze. Alternatively, transfer to a shallow metal tray and freeze, whisking every couple of hours until creamy and frozen.

NOTE: Fresh passionfruit pulp is preferable for this recipe, although it is sometimes also available frozen.

Honey & thyme ice cream

Makes 1.25 litres (44 fl oz)

12 egg yolks
175 g (6 oz/$3/4$ cup) caster (superfine) sugar
100 g (3$1/2$ oz/scant $1/3$ cup) honey
1 litre (35 fl oz/4 cups) pouring (whipping) cream
1 small bunch of thyme (about 15 g/ $1/2$ oz), leaves picked

In a bowl, lightly whisk together the egg yolks and sugar. Stir in the honey. Heat the cream and thyme leaves in a large saucepan and bring almost to the boil. Whisk the hot cream mixture into the egg yolks, then return to a clean saucepan over medium heat.

Using a wooden spoon, stir constantly until the custard thickens and coats the back of the spoon. Do not let it boil. Strain through a fine sieve, allow to cool to room temperature, then refrigerate until cold.

Transfer to an ice cream machine, churn according to the manufacturer's instructions, then freeze. Alternatively, transfer to a shallow metal tray and freeze, whisking every couple of hours until creamy and frozen.

Chocolate & hazelnut ice cream

Makes 1.25 litres (44 fl oz)

400 g (14 oz/2²/₃ cups) chopped
good-quality dark (bittersweet)
chocolate, such as couverture
6 egg yolks
150 g (5¹/₂ oz/²/₃ cup) caster
(superfine) sugar
1 vanilla bean, spilt lengthways
600 ml (21 fl oz) milk
400 ml (14 fl oz) pouring (whipping)
cream
95 g (3¹/₄ oz/²/₃ cup) hazelnuts,
roasted, skinned and roughly
chopped

Put the chocolate in a heatproof bowl over a saucepan of simmering water and allow to melt, stirring occasionally, until smooth. Remove from the heat and set aside.

In a bowl, lightly whisk together the egg yolks and sugar. Scrape the seeds from the vanilla bean into a large saucepan. Add the vanilla bean, milk and cream and bring almost to the boil. Whisk the hot milk mixture into the egg yolks, then return to a clean saucepan over medium heat.

Using a wooden spoon, stir constantly until the custard thickens and coats the back of the spoon. Do not let it boil. Strain through a fine sieve, then stir in the melted chocolate. Allow to cool to room temperature, then refrigerate until cold.

Transfer to an ice cream machine and churn according to the manufacturer's instructions. Alternatively, transfer to a shallow metal tray and freeze, whisking every couple of hours until creamy and frozen.

When nearly fully frozen, add the hazelnuts.

Caramel balsamic ice cream

Makes about 1 litre (35 fl oz)

250 g (9 oz/heaped 1 cup) caster (superfine) sugar
60 ml (2 fl oz/$^1/_4$ cup) good-quality balsamic vinegar
6 egg yolks
500 ml (17 fl oz/2 cups) milk
150 ml (5 fl oz) thick (double/heavy) cream
200 ml (7 fl oz) good-quality balsamic vinegar, extra

Combine the sugar and just enough water to cover in a small saucepan and stir until the sugar has dissolved. Bring to the boil and boil, without stirring, until the syrup becomes a light golden colour. Immediately remove from the heat and very carefully, as hot caramel spits, add the vinegar. Return to the heat and stir until smooth, then remove from the heat and allow to cool to room temperature. Refrigerate until cold.

In a bowl, lightly whisk the egg yolks. Put the milk and cream in a large saucepan and bring almost to the boil. Whisk the hot milk mixture into the egg yolks, then return to a clean saucepan over medium heat.

Using a wooden spoon, stir constantly until the custard thickens and coats the back of the spoon. Do not let it boil. Strain through a fine sieve, then allow to cool to room temperature.

Put the extra vinegar in a heavy-based saucepan over medium heat. Bring to the boil, then reduce the heat and simmer until it reduces to a syrup consistency. Remove from the heat and set aside to cool.

Whisk the cold caramel mixture into the custard. Transfer to an ice cream machine and churn according to the manufacturer's instructions. Alternatively, transfer to a shallow metal tray and freeze, whisking every couple of hours until creamy and frozen.

When nearly fully frozen, gradually pour in the reduced balsamic vinegar to give a rippled effect.

Burnt caramel ice cream with pistachio baklava wafers

Serves 6

300 g (10$^1/_2$ oz/1$^1/_3$ cups) caster
  (superfine) sugar
500 ml (17 fl oz/2 cups) milk
500 ml (17 fl oz/2 cups) pouring
  (whipping) cream
10 egg yolks

PISTACHIO BAKLAVA WAFERS
2 sheets of filo pastry
50 g (1$^3/_4$ oz) unsalted butter,
  melted
150 g (5$^1/_2$ oz/1 cup) shelled,
  unsalted pistachio nuts,
  blanched, skinned and roughly
  chopped
55 g (2 oz/$^1/_4$ cup) raw (demerara)
  sugar
$^1/_2$ teaspoon ground cinnamon

Combine 200 g (7 oz/scant 1 cup) of the sugar and 125 ml (4 fl oz/$^1/2$ cup) water in a large saucepan over medium heat and stir until the sugar has dissolved. Bring to the boil and boil, without stirring, until the syrup turns a dark golden colour. Immediately remove from the heat and very carefully, as hot caramel spits, stir in the milk and cream. Return to medium heat and bring almost to the boil.

In a bowl, lightly whisk together the egg yolks and remaining sugar. Whisk the hot milk mixture into the egg yolks, then return to a clean saucepan over medium heat.

Using a wooden spoon, stir constantly until the custard thickens and coats the back of the spoon. Do not let it boil. Strain through a fine sieve, allow to cool to room temperature, then refrigerate until cold.

Transfer to an ice cream machine, churn according to the manufacturer's instructions, then freeze. Alternatively, transfer to a shallow metal tray and freeze, whisking every couple of hours until creamy and frozen.

Preheat the oven to 180°C (350°F/Gas 4). Grease and line several baking trays with baking paper.

To make the pistachio baklava wafers, cut each sheet of filo into thirds lengthways, then lay a strip of filo pastry on a chopping board and brush with melted butter. Place another strip of pastry on top, brush with melted butter and repeat to make four layers of pastry. Brush the top with butter, then sprinkle with the chopped pistachios, sugar and cinnamon.

Cut the pastry into six triangles, place on the prepared trays and bake for 6–8 minutes, or until the pastry has risen and is golden in colour. Cool the wafers on a wire rack.

Scoop the burnt caramel ice cream into serving bowls and serve with the wafers.

Macadamia nut ice cream

Makes 1.25 litres (44 fl oz)

300 g (10½ oz/1⅓ cups) caster
  (superfine) sugar
500 ml (17 fl oz/2 cups) milk
500 ml (17 fl oz/2 cups) pouring
  (whipping) cream
10 egg yolks
320 g (11¼ oz/2 cups) unsalted
  macadamia nuts, roasted and
  roughly chopped

Combine 200 g (7 oz/scant 1 cup) of the sugar and
125 ml (4 fl oz/½ cup) water in a large saucepan over
medium heat and stir until the sugar has dissolved.
Bring to the boil and boil, without stirring, until the
syrup turns a light golden colour. Immediately remove
from the heat and very carefully, as hot caramel spits,
stir in the milk and cream. Return to medium heat
and bring almost to the boil.

In a bowl, lightly whisk together the egg yolks
and remaining sugar. Whisk in the hot milk mixture,
then return to a clean saucepan over medium heat.

Using a wooden spoon, stir constantly until the
custard thickens and coats the back of the spoon.
Do not let it boil. Strain through a fine sieve, allow to
cool to room temperature, then refrigerate until cold.

Transfer to an ice cream machine and churn
according to the manufacturer's instructions.
Alternatively, transfer to a shallow metal tray and
freeze, whisking every couple of hours until creamy
and frozen.

When nearly fully frozen, add the macadamias.

Salted peanut caramel ice cream

Makes 1.5 litres (52 fl oz)

SALTED PEANUT CARAMEL
200 g (7 oz/1$^1/_4$ cups) raw unsalted peanuts
sea salt, for sprinkling
200 ml (7 fl oz) pouring (whipping) cream
75 g (2$^1/_2$ oz/$^1/_3$ cup) glucose syrup
$^1/_2$ vanilla bean, split lengthways, seeds scraped
115 g (4 oz/$^1/_2$ cup) caster (superfine) sugar
50 g (1$^3/_4$ oz) unsalted butter, chopped

12 egg yolks
300 g (10$^1/_2$ oz/1$^1/_3$ cups) caster (superfine) sugar
2 vanilla beans, split lengthways
500 ml (17 fl oz/2 cups) milk
500 ml (17 fl oz/2 cups) pouring (whipping) cream

Preheat the oven to 180°C (350°F/Gas 4).

To make the salted peanut caramel, spread the peanuts on a baking tray, sprinkle with sea salt and roast for 5–7 minutes, or until golden. Allow to cool, then roughly chop.

Put the cream and glucose syrup in a saucepan. Scrape the seeds from the vanilla bean into the saucepan and place over medium heat. Bring to the boil, then remove from the heat.

Combine the sugar and just enough water to cover in a heavy-based saucepan over medium heat and stir until the sugar has dissolved. Bring to the boil and boil, without stirring, until the syrup becomes a dark golden colour. Immediately remove from the heat and very carefully, as hot caramel spits, add the hot cream mixture. Return to low heat and whisk in the butter, one piece at a time, and stir until the caramel is smooth. Strain through a fine sieve, then add the peanuts. Set aside to cool.

In a bowl, lightly whisk together the egg yolks and sugar. Scrape the seeds from the vanilla beans into a large saucepan. Add the vanilla beans, milk and cream and bring almost to the boil. Whisk the hot milk mixture into the egg yolks, then return to a clean saucepan over medium heat.

Using a wooden spoon, stir constantly until the custard thickens and coats the back of the spoon. Do not let it boil. Strain through a fine sieve, allow to cool to room temperature, then refrigerate until cold.

Transfer to an ice cream machine and churn according to the manufacturer's instructions. Alternatively, transfer to a shallow metal tray and freeze, whisking every couple of hours until creamy and frozen.

When nearly fully frozen, gradually add the salted peanut caramel to give a rippled effect.

Nougat sorbet, bittersweet chocolate sauce, caramel & salted peanuts

Serves 6

750 ml (26 fl oz/3 cups) milk
75 g (2$^1/_2$ oz/$^1/_3$ cup) caster
  (superfine) sugar
50 ml (1$^1/_2$ fl oz) milk, extra
1 gelatine leaf (2 g/$^1/_{16}$ oz), soaked in
  cold water and squeezed out
100 g (3$^1/_2$ oz/$^1/_3$ cup) condensed milk
125 g (4$^1/_2$ oz/scant $^1/_2$ cup) chocolate
  hazelnut spread
1 tablespoon glucose syrup

150 g (5$^1/_2$ oz/1 cup) raw unsalted
  peanuts
sea salt, for sprinkling

CHOCOLATE SAUCE
75 g (2$^1/_2$ oz/$^1/_3$ cup) caster
  (superfine) sugar
60 g (2$^1/_4$ oz/$^1/_2$ cup) grated
  good-quality dark (bittersweet)
  chocolate, such as couverture
45 g (1$^1/_2$ oz/$^1/_3$ cup) unsweetened
  cocoa powder, sifted

CARAMEL
250 g (9 oz/heaped 1 cup) 61caster
  (superfine) sugar
250 ml (9 fl oz/1 cup) pouring
  (whipping) cream, warmed

caramel shards (Basics, page 178),
  to serve

Combine the milk and sugar in a large saucepan over medium heat and stir until the sugar has dissolved. Bring to the boil and simmer until reduced by one-third. Remove from the heat.

Gently heat the extra milk in a small saucepan, then pour into a large bowl. Whisk in the softened gelatine and stir to completely dissolve. Add the condensed milk, chocolate hazelnut spread and glucose syrup and mix well to combine. Whisk in the reduced milk mixture, allow to cool to room temperature, then refrigerate until cold.

Transfer to an ice cream machine, churn according to the manufacturer's instructions, then freeze. Alternatively, transfer to a shallow metal tray and freeze, whisking every couple of hours until creamy and frozen.

Preheat the oven to 180°C (350°F/Gas 4). Spread the peanuts on a baking tray, sprinkle with sea salt and roast for 5–7 minutes, or until golden. Allow to cool, then roughly chop. Store in an airtight container until required.

To make the chocolate sauce, combine the sugar and 400 ml (14 fl oz) water in a small saucepan over low heat and stir until the sugar has dissolved. Stir in the chocolate and cocoa powder and simmer for 10 minutes, stirring occasionally. Remove from the heat and strain through a fine sieve into a pouring jug. Set aside to cool to room temperature.

To make the caramel, combine the sugar and 60 ml (2 fl oz/$^1/4$ cup) water in a small saucepan over medium heat and stir until the sugar has dissolved. Bring to the boil and boil, without stirring, until the syrup becomes a light golden colour. Immediately remove from the heat and very carefully, as hot caramel spits, stir in the cream. Return to the heat and stir until the caramel is smooth. Set aside to cool.

To serve, scoop the nougat sorbet into the centre of serving bowls. Pour the chocolate sauce around the sorbet and drizzle with the caramel. Scatter the peanuts around and top with caramel shards.

Coffee chocolate ice cream

Makes about 1 litre (35 fl oz)

100 ml (3$^1/_2$ fl oz) hot espresso
 or strong plunger coffee
50 g (1$^3/_4$ oz/$^1/_3$ cup) chopped
 good-quality dark (bittersweet)
 chocolate, such as couverture
2 tablespoons Tia Maria
6 egg yolks
80 g (2$^3/_4$ oz/$^1/_3$ cup) caster
 (superfine) sugar
500 ml (17 fl oz/2 cups) pouring
 (whipping) cream
50 g (1$^3/_4$ oz) glucose syrup

Put the coffee, chocolate and Tia Maria in a large bowl and set aside.

In a bowl, lightly whisk together the egg yolks and sugar. Heat the cream and glucose syrup in a large saucepan over medium heat, stirring to melt the glucose syrup, and bring almost to the boil. Whisk the hot cream mixture into the egg yolks, then return to a clean saucepan over medium heat.

Using a wooden spoon, stir constantly until the custard thickens and coats the back of the spoon. Do not let it boil. Pour the custard over the coffee and chocolate mixture, stirring to melt the chocolate. Strain through a fine sieve, allow to cool to room temperature, then refrigerate until cold.

Transfer to an ice cream machine, churn according to the manufacturer's instructions, then freeze. Alternatively, transfer to a shallow metal tray and freeze, whisking every couple of hours until creamy and frozen.

Mint chocolate ice cream

Makes 1.25 litres (44 fl oz)

400 g (14 oz/1^3/$_4$ cups) caster
  (superfine) sugar
250 g (9 oz/1^2/$_3$ cups) chopped
  good-quality white chocolate,
  such as couverture
75 ml (2^3/$_4$ fl oz) crème de menthe
1^1/$_2$ tablespoons vodka
200 g (7 oz/1^1/$_3$ cups) chopped
  good-quality dark (bittersweet)
  chocolate, such as couverture

Combine the sugar and 400 ml (14 fl oz) water in a saucepan over medium heat and stir until the sugar has dissolved. Bring to the boil, then reduce the heat and simmer for 2 minutes. Remove the sugar syrup from the heat and set aside to cool.

Put the white chocolate in a heavy-based saucepan over low heat, stirring occasionally, until the chocolate just melts. Add the crème de menthe, vodka and 600 ml (21 fl oz) water and stir until well combined. Bring to the boil, then remove from the heat.

Stir in the sugar syrup, allow to cool to room temperature, then refrigerate until cold. Transfer to an ice cream machine and churn according to the manufacturer's instructions. Alternatively, transfer to a shallow metal tray and freeze, whisking every couple of hours until creamy and frozen.

When nearly fully frozen, mix in the chopped dark chocolate.

BASICS

Here you'll find some basic recipes used throughout this book.
Straightforward and simple, most can be made well ahead of time
and whipped out at the last minute to add flair to even
the simplest dessert.

Balsamic syrup

Makes about 250 ml (9 fl oz/1 cup)

400 ml (14 fl oz) good-quality
   balsamic vinegar
100 g (3$^1/_2$ oz/scant $^1/_2$ cup) caster
   (superfine) sugar

Put the balsamic vinegar and sugar in a small saucepan over medium heat and stir until the sugar has dissolved. Bring to the boil, then reduce the heat and simmer until the liquid has reduced to a syrup consistency. Set aside to cool, then transfer to an airtight container and refrigerate until required. The syrup will keep refrigerated for several days.

NOTE: Balsamic syrup is wonderful with berry and chocolate desserts as the acidity of the vinegar helps to balance the sweetness of the sugar. Only use in small amounts as the flavour is very strong.

Biscotti

Makes 30–40

300 g (10$^1/_2$ oz) plain (all-purpose)
   flour, sifted
270 g (9$^1/_2$ oz/scant 1$^1/_4$ cups) caster
   (superfine) sugar
$^3/_4$ teaspoon baking powder
2 eggs
2 egg yolks
$^3/_4$ teaspoon natural vanilla extract
grated zest of $^1/_2$ orange
grated zest of $^1/_2$ lemon
135 g (4$^3/_4$ oz/scant 1 cup) whole
   unblanched almonds

Preheat the oven to 160°C (315°F/Gas 2–3). Grease and line a baking tray with baking paper.

Combine the flour, sugar and baking powder in a large mixing bowl, then make a well in the centre. In a separate bowl, whisk together the eggs, egg yolks, vanilla extract, orange zest and lemon zest. Add to the dry ingredients, gently mix to combine, then add the almonds.

On a floured surface, form the mixture into a rectangular shape measuring about 30 x 10 cm (12 x 4 inches). Place on the prepared tray, making sure the shape is well formed and firm. Bake for 35 minutes, or until golden, then remove from the oven and allow to cool completely.

Preheat the oven to 80°C (175°F/Gas $^1/_4$). Line several baking trays with baking paper.

Cut the biscotti into very thin slices, about 2–3 mm ($^1/_8$ inch) thick, and lay flat on the prepared trays. Return to the oven and slowly dry the biscotti for 1–2 hours, or until very crisp, checking the biscotti occasionally. Remove from the oven and allow to cool. Biscotti will keep for several days in an airtight container.

NOTE: You can use any combination of nuts (such as hazelnuts and pistachios) for this recipe. Simply substitute the same weight of nuts as the almonds.

Blind-baked sweet shortcrust pastry

Makes one 24 x 4 cm (9$^1/_2$ x 1$^1/_2$ inch) pastry case, or six 8 x 2 cm (3$^1/_4$ x $^3/_4$ inch) tartlet cases

150 g (5$^1/_2$ oz) unsalted butter,
   at room temperature
100 g (3$^1/_2$ oz/heaped $^3/_4$ cup) icing
   (confectioners') sugar
1 egg yolk
250 g (9 oz) plain (all-purpose) flour
1 egg, beaten

Cream the butter and icing sugar together in a food processor. Add the egg yolk, mix well, then add the flour — do not overwork. If necessary, add just enough chilled water to bring the pastry together on the blade. Knead lightly, then wrap in plastic wrap and refrigerate for 1 hour.

Roll out the pastry 3 mm ($^1/_8$ inch) thick and gently ease into a greased 24 x 4 cm (9$^1/_2$ x 1$^1/_2$ inch) tart tin, or six 8 x 2 cm (3$^1/_4$ x $^3/_4$ inch) tartlet tins. Refrigerate for a further 30 minutes. (If you are making the pastry ahead of time, place it in the freezer until required. There is no need to thaw frozen pastry cases before using.)

To blind-bake the pastry, preheat the oven to 180°C (350°F/Gas 4). Cover the base and sides of the pastry case or tartlet cases with baking paper or foil, then fill with pastry weights (such as baking beads, uncooked rice or split peas). Bake for 10–12 minutes. Remove the pastry weights and lining, brush with the beaten egg and bake for a further 5–8 minutes, or until golden. Use as recipe directs.

Candied walnuts

Makes about 2 cups

200 g (7 oz/scant 1 cup) caster
   (superfine) sugar
200 g (7 oz/2 cups) walnuts

Set a wire rack over a baking tray. Combine the sugar and 60 ml (2 fl oz/$^1/_4$ cup) water in a heavy-based saucepan over medium heat and stir until the sugar has dissolved. Bring to the boil and boil, without stirring, until the syrup becomes a dark golden colour. Immediately remove from the heat and add all the walnuts at once.

Quickly pour the mixture onto the wire rack and use a spoon to carefully spread the nuts in an even layer — the caramel will be very hot. Allow to cool completely, then store in an airtight container until required.

Caramel shards

Makes about 1 cup

230 g (8 oz/1 cup) caster (superfine) sugar

Grease and line a baking tray with baking paper.

Combine the sugar and 80 ml ($2^1/_2$ fl oz/$^1/_3$ cup) water in a saucepan over medium heat and stir until the sugar has dissolved. Bring to the boil and boil, without stirring, until the syrup turns a dark golden colour. Immediately remove from the heat.

Quickly pour the mixture over the prepared tray and flatten out using the back of a hot metal spoon. Allow to cool. Once cold, break the caramel into shards.

Caramel shards will keep for several days in an airtight container — do not refrigerate.

Crème anglaise

Makes about 625 ml ($21^1/_2$ fl oz/$2^1/_2$ cups)

3 egg yolks
55 g (2 oz/$^1/_4$ cup) caster (superfine) sugar
$^1/_2$ vanilla bean, split lengthways
250 ml (9 fl oz/1 cup) milk
250 ml (9 fl oz/1 cup) pouring (whipping) cream

Lightly whisk the egg yolks and sugar together in a bowl. Scrape the seeds from the vanilla bean into a saucepan. Add the vanilla bean, milk and cream and bring almost to the boil. Whisk the hot milk mixture into the egg mixture, then return to a clean saucepan over medium heat.

Using a wooden spoon, stir constantly until the custard thickens and coats the back of the spoon. Do not let it boil. Strain through a fine sieve, allow to cool to room temperature, then refrigerate until cold.

Crème anglaise will keep refrigerated for one or two days and can also be served warm with warm puddings. To serve warm, gently reheat in a saucepan over low heat.

Cherry syrup

Makes about 250 ml (9 fl oz/1 cup)

115 g (4 oz/$^1/_2$ cup) caster (superfine)
   sugar
grated zest of $^1/_2$ lemon
1 vanilla bean, spilt lengthways,
   seeds scraped
250 g (9 oz) cherries, pitted, stems
   removed

Combine the sugar and 125 ml (4 fl oz/$^1/_2$ cup) water in a heavy-based saucepan over medium heat and stir until the sugar has dissolved. Add the lemon zest, vanilla bean and vanilla seeds and bring to the boil. Reduce the heat, then add the cherries and simmer for 6–10 minutes, stirring occasionally, until the cherries are soft. Remove from the heat and set aside to cool.

Once the syrup has cooled, remove the vanilla bean, then transfer the syrup to a blender and blend until smooth. The syrup will keep for several days refrigerated in an airtight container.

Gingerbread

Makes 10–12 wedges

75 g (2$^1/_2$ oz) unsalted butter,
   softened
125 g (4$^1/_2$ oz/heaped $^1/_2$ cup) caster
   (superfine) sugar
1 tablespoon golden syrup or light
   corn syrup
1 teaspoon ground ginger
2 teaspoons ground cinnamon
$^1/_4$ teaspoon ground cloves
$^1/_2$ teaspoon ground cardamom
1 teaspoon bicarbonate of soda
   (baking soda)
1$^1/_2$ tablespoons milk
250 g (9 oz) plain (all-purpose) flour,
   sifted

Put the butter, sugar, golden syrup, spices and bicarbonate of soda in the bowl of an electric mixer and beat until well combined. Gradually pour in the milk and 1 tablespoon water, mixing well to combine, then slowly add the flour. Shape the dough into a flattened ball, wrap in plastic wrap and refrigerate for at least 1 hour.

Preheat the oven to 180°C (350°F/Gas 4). Grease and line a baking tray with baking paper.

On a lightly floured surface, roll out the rested gingerbread 1–2 mm ($^1/_{16}$ inch) thick. Using a large dinner plate as a stencil, cut the gingerbread into a large circle, then into 10 wedges. (If it's easier, you could cut the circle into 12 wedges, and save two wedges to enjoy another time.) Carefully lift each wedge onto the prepared tray, then bake for 10–12 minutes, or until golden.

Allow to cool completely on a wire rack, then store in an airtight container. The gingerbread will keep for several days.

Poached quince

Serves 6

1 kg (2 lb 4 oz/4$^1/_3$ cups) caster
  (superfine) sugar
juice of 3 lemons
2 cinnamon sticks
2 star anise
6 cloves
1 vanilla bean, split lengthways,
  seeds scraped
6 quinces

Combine the sugar and 2 litres (70 fl oz/8 cups) water in a heavy-based saucepan over medium heat and stir until the sugar has dissolved. Add the lemon juice, cinnamon sticks, star anise, cloves, vanilla bean and vanilla seeds and bring to the boil.

Peel each quince, cut them into quarters and remove the cores. Add the quince, cores and skins to the saucepan (the skins and cores will give the poached fruit a brilliant red colour). Reduce the heat to low and gently simmer for 1–1$^1/_2$ hours, or until the quince is tender. Remove from the heat and allow the quince to cool in the poaching syrup.

Using a slotted spoon, carefully remove the quince quarters from the syrup and transfer to a plastic container. Strain the syrup, discarding the skins, cores and spices, then pour over the quince quarters.

Poached quince will keep refrigerated in the syrup for 1–2 days. Use as recipe directs.

NOTE: Poached quince also makes a simple and delicious winter dessert. Gently reheat the poached quinces in their syrup and serve with custard or cream. The syrup can also be drizzled over desserts for added flavour.

Raspberry coulis

Makes about 125 ml (4 fl oz/$\frac{1}{2}$ cup)

1 tablespoon honey
115 g (4 oz/$\frac{1}{2}$ cup) caster (superfine)
   sugar
juice of 1 lime
200 g (7 oz) fresh or frozen raspberries
   (see Note)

Combine the honey, sugar and lime juice in a small saucepan over medium heat and stir until the sugar has dissolved. Bring to the boil, then add the raspberries and cook at a rapid boil for 1 minute. Remove from the heat and cool slightly.

Transfer to a food processor and blend until smooth. Strain through a fine sieve. Raspberry coulis will keep for several days in an airtight container in the refrigerator.

NOTE: Frozen raspberries can be added straight from the freezer. Drizzle any left-over raspberry coulis over desserts and ice creams, or store in the freezer for up to six weeks.

Tuiles

Makes about 20

25 g (1 oz) unsalted butter, softened
55 g (2 oz/$\frac{1}{4}$ cup) caster (superfine)
   sugar
55 g (2 oz) plain (all-purpose) flour
2 egg whites

In the bowl of an electric mixer, cream the butter and sugar together until light and pale. Add the flour and egg whites, beating until smooth. Refrigerate the tuile mixture for 1 hour before using.

Preheat the oven to 160°C (315°F/Gas 2–3). Draw three 10 cm (4 inch) circles on baking paper and invert the paper over a baking tray. Repeat with another sheet of baking paper and baking tray.

Using a spatula, smear a thin layer of the tuile mixture onto each circle and bake for 3–5 minutes, or until brown at the edges and golden in the centre.

Remove from the oven and, working quickly using a clean palette knife or spatula, carefully remove one tuile and shape it by placing over a rolling pin to curl. Repeat with the second and third tuile — they should all fit on the one rolling pin. If they become too hard to remove, return the tray briefly to the oven to soften.

Repeat the process with the remaining tuile mixture. Allow to cool, then store in an airtight container until required. The tuiles will keep for several days.

Sesame wafers

Makes about 20

80 g (2³/₄ oz/¹/₃ cup) caster
  (superfine) sugar
zest of 1 orange
2 tablespoons freshly squeezed
  orange juice
40 g (1¹/₂ oz) plain (all-purpose) flour
¹/₄ teaspoon ground ginger
40 g (1¹/₂ oz/¹/₄ cup) sesame seeds
40 g (1¹/₂ oz) unsalted butter,
  melted
1 tablespoon finely chopped glacé
  ginger

In a bowl, combine the sugar, orange zest and orange juice and stir until the sugar has dissolved.

In a separate bowl, sift together the flour and ground ginger, then add the sesame seeds. Make a well in the centre and stir in the melted butter and the orange mixture, mixing well to combine. Lastly add the glacé ginger. Refrigerate the wafer mixture for 1 hour before using.

Preheat the oven to 170°C (325°F/Gas 3). Draw three 8 cm (3¹/4 inch) circles on a sheet of baking paper and invert the paper over a baking tray. Repeat with another sheet of baking paper and baking tray.

Using a spatula, smear a thin layer of wafer mixture onto each circle and bake for 7–10 minutes, or until golden. Slide the sheets of baking paper onto a wire rack and allow the wafers to cool completely before removing. Repeat the process with the remaining wafer mixture.

Sesame wafers will keep for several days in an airtight container.

Walnut praline

Makes about 3 cups

500 g (1 lb 2 oz/2 heaped cups) caster
  (superfine) sugar
250 g (9 oz/2¹/₂ cups) walnuts

Grease and line a baking tray with baking paper. Combine the sugar and just enough water to cover in a heavy-based saucepan over medium heat and stir until the sugar has dissolved. Bring to the boil and boil, without stirring, until the syrup becomes a dark golden colour. Immediately remove from the heat and add all the walnuts at once.

Quickly pour the mixture over the prepared tray and flatten out using the back of a hot metal spoon. Allow to cool. Once cold, break into pieces. Store in an airtight container until required.

Glossary

Blanching pistachios
To remove the skins from pistachios, put the nuts in a small saucepan with enough water to cover, bring to the boil and boil for several minutes. Drain and rub in a clean tea towel (dish towel) to remove the skins. Spread out on a dry surface to cool completely before storing in a sealed container.

Botrytis
Botrytis cinerea, also referred to as noble rot, is a beneficial mould or fungus that attacks grapes under certain climatic conditions and causes them to shrivel, deeply concentrating the flavours, sugar and acid. Some of the most famous examples come from Sauternes (Château d'Yquem), Germany and Tokay.

Brioche
A soft, sweet leavened bread enriched with eggs.

Couverture
Good-quality chocolate with a high proportion of cocoa butter. It should melt easily on the tongue and not leave a fatty residue on the roof of the mouth. Avoid compound cooking chocolate.

Cream
Creaming butter and sugar is the technique of beating the two together to dissolve the sugar crystals. The mixture will become pale in colour and aerated.

Crème fraîche
A distinctively sharp, semi-sour cream that can be substituted for sour cream.

Dariole moulds
Round, flat-bottomed moulds with flared sides, available in aluminium, stainless steel and plastic in 125 ml (4 fl oz/^{1}/$_2$ cup), 150 ml (5 fl oz) and 180 ml (6 fl oz) capacity. Plastic ones are good for cold puddings such as panna cotta, as their flexibility makes it easier to turn out the dessert.

Gelatine
One teaspoon gelatine powder is equal to 3.5 g of gelatine leaves, so to substitute a 4 g (^{1}/$_8$ oz) gelatine leaf, dissolve 1 heaped teaspoon in an equal amount of cold water. This will form a jelly that can be added to hot liquid, as you would with gelatine leaves. Leaf gelatine is sold in good delicatessens and is superior to gelatine powder.

Glucose syrup
Glucose syrup, made from corn, has about half the sweetening power of sugar. Due to its molecular make-up it doesn't crystallise; this makes it popular in the making of sweets and frostings.

Knock down (or punch back)
After an initial rising, yeasted dough is knocked down or punched back to deflate it. This redistributes the yeast, releases excess carbon dioxide and evens the temperature before the dough is shaped.

Mandolin
A manual stainless steel slicing utensil, used for very finely and uniformly slicing any firm fruits or vegetables.

Praline
Caramel combined with nuts, then crushed.

Ramekins
Small ceramic pots that come in various sizes and are used for baking.

Sauternes
This small wine region in Bordeaux, France, produces grapes affected by botrytis, a mould that causes ripe grapes to shrivel, yielding a very concentrated juice. The term generally refers to sweet dessert wines.

Soft-ball stage
A method of testing sugar syrup to see if it has boiled to the right temperature. When a small amount of the boiling syrup is dropped into cold water, it will form a soft, gummy ball when rolled between your fingers, though it flattens out on its own once removed from the water. On a sugar thermometer, the sugar syrup should reach at least 112°C (233°F), but no more than 120°C (248°F).

Strong flour
Flour of any type made from hard wheat which has a high protein (gluten) content. It is used mainly in bread-making and for puff and choux pastry.

Index

Published in 2008 by Murdoch Books Pty Limited

Murdoch Books Australia
Pier 8/9
23 Hickson Road
Millers Point NSW 2000
Phone: +61 (0) 2 8220 2000
Fax: +61 (0) 2 8220 2558
www.murdochbooks.com.au

Murdoch Books UK L imited
Erico House, 6th Floor
93-99 Upper Richmond Road
Putney, London SW15 2TG
Phone: +44 (0) 20 8785 5995
Fax: +44 (0) 20 8785 5985
www.murdochbooks.co.uk

Chief Executive: Juliet Rogers
Publishing Director: Kay Scarlett

Editor: Katri Hilden
Food editor: Joanne Glynn
Design manager: Vivien Valk
Concept and design: Anne Barton
Photographer: Jared Fowler
Stylist: Cherise Koch
Production: Tiffany Johnson
Special thanks to Kova Pty Ltd, 23 James St, Fortitude Valley, Brisbane, for generously supplying the
Mud Ceramics crockery for photography.

e'cco
100 Boundary St
(cnr Adelaide St)
Brisbane Qld 4000
ph + 61 7 3831 8344
fax + 61 7 3831 8460
mail@eccobistro.com
www.eccobistro.com

Text copyright (c) 2008 Philip Johnson
Photography and design copyright (c) 2008 Murdoch Books

National Library of Australia Cataloguing-in-Publication Data
Johnson, Philip, 1959- .
Decadence.

Includes index.
ISBN 9781921259500 (hbk.).

    1. Écco (Restaurant). 2. Desserts. I. Title.

    641.86

A catalogue record for this book is available from the British Library.

Colour separation by Splitting Image Colour Studio, Melbourne, Australia.
Printed by Midas Printing (Asia) Ltd.

IMPORTANT: Those who might be at risk from the effects of salmonella poisoning (the elderly, pregnant
women, young children and those suffering from immune deficiency diseases) should consult their doctor with
any concerns about eating raw eggs.

CONVERSION GUIDE: You may find cooking times vary depending on the oven you are using. For fan-forced
ovens, as a general rule, set the oven temperature to 20°C (35°F) lower than indicated in the recipe. We have
used 20 ml (4 teaspoon) tablespoon measures. If you are using a 15 ml (3 teaspoon) tablespoon, for most
recipes the difference will not be noticeable. However, for recipes using baking powder, gelatine, bicarbonate
of soda (baking soda), small amounts of flour and cornflour (cornstarch), add an extra teaspoon for each
tablespoon specified.